D0969860

THE BROKEN BURN

AC CALLOWAY

To the Demons
 who have ravaged me
 and to the
 Angels
 who were my Saviors

part one

In the safety of the branches
he felt the tremble of the earth
the burn of the leaves the
fire all around him.

Torch

This night of mystic

the curtains flutter at the window with
a gush of night air.
the flicker of candle light
and then he is
there ~ standing
a
glow
of white
against the red
his eyes fixed solid on me
as I
lay motionless in the
shadows.
I close my book
and
pull up on my
pillow.

this room where you dwell
filled with passion is
a sacred space.

his voice
a
grumble
his wicked smile
intense
his
presence
intoxicating
lurking from the
dark
black corner
of my room.

what do you want
I whisper.
my voice
low and broken

the scent of
musk
swirling around him
and my head
grows dizzy.

all of his whiteness
in all of my red
I am not prepared
to see.
there is a buzz
to the light,
bright and dark somehow
at the same time
and I say

I have not been ready
these years past
yet
some how I knew
this day would be.

your leather bound book
your collection of words
I am here to read

his eyes
the darkest brown
his breath warm
drifting across the room
over my bed
to me
over me
inside of me.

no, thank you
I say
those writings, I wish to be left
alone.

that is past
healing is my only concern.

stay away from me
go
now
leave.

he moves closer

you have done well.

he says
again a heavy whisper
again
that
smile
and then
his hands
are somehow holding my leather bound
book
that I had
placed in the wooden box
at the end of my bed
where only I have
the key

say yes.

he taunts me
knowing he will get
what he wants

~ that I may open this
and read over black roses.
he says,
allow
me to
read
the words as I see you here.
pray for rain,
and then
I will go.
not forever
but, I will

go where the haunted stay

his smile is gone
his hands solid on my book
the red paper walls
the red cotton and silk on the bed
they grow
warm
and I do not feel safe
and I know I have no
words
to say
that will make this spirit man
go away
and so
I
tell
him
yes ~ read my words
if that is what you have come
to do.

the candles dim
the musk scent swirls
the memory of
black roses
over power
my mind

he opens the book
and
with a sardonic grin,
he begins to read…

At the broken down damn

One afternoon grief seemed beaten with the tiny
yellow blossoms I held in my hand. It is going
to be alright I told myself and also, I told you.
Your pain doubled, it ran deep to your bone and
the tears you cried were for the others. For the
lost and damaged and the broken.

You approached from over the hills where the
valleys were warm and green. Blinded and
hot to the touch and when the sunset, the
screams, the blackness ~ so complete. Earth
cold and dark where sap stuck to our hands, our
knees, our souls waiting for the light.

Then the crocus on the day trip where the
snow had melted and again, the green, lush
valley. You smiled that golden and took my hand
and promised we would make it there ~ our
journey to honesty and light and the last place
for home along the brooks of broken damns.

The Farm

I drive
up the lane
past the plum orchard
to the old farm house.
I look
for you
on the porch.
Think of you
out plowing the field
in the dark.
My
headlights flash over
your tire swing
that hangs
from the giant oak.
You
are nowhere in sight.
In the cold
I stand
by the barn
I wait
I long for your touch
think of your voice
inside the house,
on your old fat bed
of feathers
making love
while
on the radio
the farm market report
and you're mumbling
whispers
in my ear,
your calloused hands
that smell of dairy and hogs,
the barbed wire cuts
that I tend to
peroxide, a cotton bandage.
I clip your hair

by the sink on Sunday mornings.
I watch you brush your teeth at
night before lights out
and the curtains
dance
at the window
and I sleep in this fat bed
with the glory of you
making love
and sleep
and love
and sleep
and in the morning you are gone when I wake
busy out in the barn.
I drink coffee and leave you a note.
I dress and I drive
back in to town
as the silver morning sky
turns to light
and I cherish
oh
how I
cherish
my time with you on
the farm.

Clearing Cloudberry

as you step into this journey, keep your head thoughts
clear. plenty of water with bowls of fresh berries and
every morning ~ *the wine.*

hold thoughts up ~ *boldly,* to the light.
dark blue stains, red veins, hand held ~ *secrets.*
bellies full ~ of *juicy dreams*, over cotton sheets with
spills from human flesh and blackberries under foot as
you stand ~ as you step ~ raspberry juice ~ *down your thighs.*
in your head ~ agony softens ~ blueberries heal the mind as

your dreams shift to a world where ~ the sharp tongues of the
elders and the elderberries are waiting.

cover you in linen, honey, strawberries ~ *persimmons*
currants on your tongue
gooseberries
solace
rage
and drink
every night ~ as in morning ~ *the wine*

and berries, berries ~ fistfuls of berries!

sweet gypsy
you
and you do understand, you are no longer
unacceptably
out of bounds
you have been reclaimed, romanticized, shroud in mystery.

wild gypsy lover, my soul of passion who never wanted
your salutation, that *scoff* ~ it's meaning.
yet
you
lit the fire in my imagination
and now I
will not
let you go

clean berries, fresh berries, baked berries!

my barbarian gypsy out in the woods
speak out or keep it as yours and yours
       and
           yours and yours

and you are in a wild thicket of the blackest berries
       with your ~ tangled ~ hand held ~ *secrets.*

secrets that
       are mine
             and yours and yours and yours and yours

Already the end

Drink with me this whiskey. While I think of ways to let
you go, forever: Ways to say goodbye. Lost in this run from
the bloom of colors we were promised. The rings of dreams
that went on forever, where the tower of time on the clock
screams "IT'S OVER" Shouts that spill the whiskey.
But how do I leave well enough alone when *I love you.*

Crush me, *damn it!* Pluck the melon from the vine.
Love runs out. I lose myself, I lose my mind. I was what
you wanted. You were my need, but then, the lust for others,
excitement. The want for new, different, not my whiskey, but
fresh, new cock, a kissing face. You oughta know, I meant
my words, my fucks, my holds. I was true to heart, bleeding

down my body to the grave in the ground. Down, down,
to the dark, cold, dirt of the earth. Screams and shouts
loud enough to spill the whiskey, break the glass, grind
to my mind where you will always be. My love. Forever.
I too will find the colors of another and drink their gin.
But it will take time. That broken clock tower of time.

Corner stone

stepping up from my grave to see the morning
light
to a bank of colored roses
I walk through the hills where the morning fog
leaves my trail

and people say they swear they saw me
floating through the stones like an angel
when I was never called that while I was living
now a ghost, a spirit, the essence of pure vigor

my mystery finally solidified to the school children
passing on the bus

to the preacher who calls it a miracle
to my uncle who says he does not believe

I watch and move through the world until dusk
gather new thoughts while other ones fade
to linger and frolic in the afternoon light

returning to my grave as the sun goes down
and the ghouls living next door awaken

Anaconda

the stairs were still covered in snow from
my walk up two hours before
in my heavy coat, my hat, my gloves.
I stepped down
thinking of the last time I saw her and
wondering when she next would call
would she be there tonight?
I knew the answer yet, still, I set on my way to see.

On the street, Anaconda was quiet. My boots
wet in the white, down the sidewalk to JFK.
In the bar, on my stool, I ordered a Jameson, took
off my coat while looking around, pretending not to
see, that
she was not there
and
Oh my god how I wanted her to be.

Mr. Levine sat down the bar, he gave a nod and a wave.
I said hello. I sat, I drank my James, I ordered another.
Mitch, the bartender turned up the tv
he was watching the fight.
I downed my drink and ordered another
waiting
wanting
needing her
to walk through that door
my life ~ now a trap in the snow
wet in white, wet in white, wanting her here
no matter how
I can not let go
I
can not STOP
thinking of her
about her…
the school teacher who makes me smile

my life ~ now a trap in the snow, wet in white,
wanting her. while I wonder
will she
will she ever
leave

        him

that husband who no longer gives her his touch
he shows no appreciation, could never want her
or love her, need her, as I do.

I curse my life
my heart, now awake,

               fell in love with a
woman

    I

      can not have

A woman, I keep wanting
and hoping and needing and

                 wanting and needing

will she
will she
ever

For her

by the window where the view remains
snow falls and I do not see her
she thinks of me, I am sure
and she longs for my touch
chalk in her hand as she also
looks past pupils to the snow outside
and under her breath
she says my name
she longs for my wanting, I long for
her kiss and that look in her eyes that
tells me to remain
pacing the floor with whiskey in my blood
and my heart thumps, calls out, over and over
for her

Her thoughts

lost in the desires that have led me to
my angish
to a man I may not possess
a husband who trusts me and who believes
when ~ while holding me in his arms
his body that turns cold
to a touch I feel ~ now warm
that I long for but must forget
how my weakness has destroyed me
my existence, the constant in my mind
my peace gone forever, and I will never
love either man again

I want no man in my heart, I do not
want desire, weakness that leads to
horrors of the soul

peace I do want, but not the pain from either man

both who claim they must possess me

Jelly fish

Close in the night where blankets are not needed
the moonlight softens the already burning fire
that falls forward from our control. Far off in the
sky a rocket going to Mars, filled inside with sailors
who will never return. You say you wish to
be on board and I beg you not to leave the Earth.

Not while I am here in the moonlight in my space suit
made from stars. Your kiss of rage as the rocket
roars and we run down to the water, splashing the
waves, glowing in the rip and the sting of love with
the burn of the jelly fish; screaming out in the sand
screaming out for relief and for more.

Bonfires of wood and smoke mark the beach.
Barefoot and naked, we fall to the shore, together.
'It is a life time to Mars.' you tell me
'So let us dream of the adventure and for you.'
you say, 'We will bring a baby tree. A tiny oak or a
spruce, so Earth will always be with you.'

Dancing bird

Down from the wire
little bird of blue, red and green.
My heart to your flight and the
rage of the fire where little
cups of piss drip in to tea
and we all sip as you fly.

Wishing for cake and kisses
to the lips of the Ruby Bellied Rude
but not to me, and not to him
where your kisses missed, are sent
to the wind.
So none when they cut down your nest.

Letting go the wash I can not have and moving
on to a kind lover
who says to me and always,
I want you.
While sunshine lifts through the branch
and each one of us wonder, where have
all the birds gone?

Midwestern dream

Past the rows of corn and blue sky, where I am sorry
for what happened to you and I, we both stand in the rubble.
It is complicated, we both agree. Both hearts completely broken.
A storm that will not pass. A day of the week we can not
remember. And the time, what is the time? It has gone and will
never return. Hearts damaged, here, where the rapid

tornado has torn through this place a family once called home.
The tractor sits in the field, the porch swing tipped over. The
house calls for a coat of paint. White and white-wash only to
later wish we were in color. Laundry dries on the line. The
screen door opens and there you stand and then an extraordinary
possibility occurs to me ~ what if we ~ were to stay together?

To make this work - We could do this, you and I. You look in
my eyes, step down from the porch and pace to removing the
clothing. Dropping to a basket, the clean wash no longer soiled,
fresh and ready to go again. My thoughts I hold together. My
thoughts I drift to the wind. You do not care to hear my desires
anymore, but in my heart I will not lose you.

along a highway in Indiana

we pull to the intersection in our
blue chevy
my dad tells me to crack
the window
so I
pound
I
pound
the glass

my sister takes my crayons and my
mom tells me to stop
before I break the window

I roll the window down to the wheels on the highway

the *Waves of Water ~ that follow me ~ along the
ditches as we drive*
                    have stopped

my parents close their eyes and nap
as I keep my undivided attention on
the passing
dark
ditch
where
*the Water and Waves
Watch*

my sister colors in her book, red and green

I fall asleep with Pink Ears, my toy bear
his blue fur against my cheek
he whispers to me
*so many secrets
that I must not tell*
and
the Water Waves

that follow
spin and swirl around me
swirl, splash and
spin
swirl
   around
          around
   around
the
four door blue chevy
around
spin
my teddy bear
around, around
spin
around

a Whirlpool of *Waves of Water*
they tip
the car
they Wave, they rock
spin, they Wave, they rock

and I wake
as my sister slumbers

and a Trucker in heavy black boots

walks up to our car

he looks in through the crack in the glass
to my sleeping parents

he looks me in the eye
he turns
away
he walks as

I watch him go

the Waves of Waters that follow me

now
follow him
  swirling   each step around
him
they spin around

yet

I know
as always

the Wild Waters flow ~ will return

as they always have
along the highway
down the ditch
of wild grass
and back

to me

While on the Winfield

down to the red creek where the green wild weeds
bend over
          they drink from the fresh water stream

while the farm duck waddles across the yard
          he thinks of beetles and wooly worms
chasing them down to gobble.

Sweet Pony Girl rides her little pony, Dolly
          crossing the gravel road to the barn
they gallop through the black eyed susans and the blazing stars.

they were sweet summers that lingered long in
sunny warm dreams
          where
pretty Tom-Boy-Bea and little Stan-the-Man
          would wade through the
briar thickets with metal buckets and plastic pails

picking, picking, picking, blackberries

pricking their skin but never their spirit

picking, picking, picking, more berries

as many as their little hands could hold
                    filling a metal bucket
                    filling a plastic pail.

across pastures, over gates, up the hill past the pony,
the chickens in their coop, the bees in the barn, the camomile
yard

to mom who is also Aunt Judy
          who
               did wash and cook those berries, turning
               them to jam
wax tops, metal seals on mason jars with homemade labels

sitting on shelves for seasons to come
                              a project well worth the fight.

the wave of memories of summer

running wild through weeds, red creeks with a story book pony.

hot toast
                    melted butter

              and the tang of blackberry jam.

pages flipping in the wind
                        the wild
                tender days of childhood behind
                        young children
                        running free
          on Seda and Anslem's farm and but for

                        the faded
                        failing
                        vail

                        we
                        can
                        never
                        go
                        back
                        there
                        again

Piston glory

the truck drivers stand in the middle of the road
watching, grinning, scheming, while sunlight fades over hills.

they drink their coffee and climb
                    behind the wheel
running cars, vans and busses off the road to
burn them with great elation ~ the ditch dug shallow.

                    tossing bottles of piss and gasoline

they stop in diners and tell their stories
scoring whores to their cabs they sleep in the cacoon of their
rigs.

18 wheels of American glory
wiping their ass with a faded flag

playing cowboys and indians at a time it is lost
no one plays those games
                    anymore
                there are new games in town with nasty.

I drive down this highway
                who am I to care

what dreams scatter to be broken

rusty rigs, wrecked pistons, burning flags, with loads of hate
and gallons of diesel 2 burn

Grenades

The armies hold the maps to blood.
Guns and grenades in boxes under beds
where monsters lurk in the human soul
and children cry at night, with their parents.
Shaking hearts and trembling hands
love smothered in blankets of yarn.

Stand up to the breeze bunkers of hate
you who are wet and shake from the cold,
you stop crying, build a new start on the day
drop clean towels in hallways, plant food,
wait at the door with brandy 4 all
of these are yours.

Thankful, you gather the young ones around you.
Your families twitch and turn in coffins while you sleep,
where the bombs have hit the head and your
imagination is all you hope to cling too,
while monsters wait in the human soul
and the rest, with secret boxes under beds.

Another season

he walks out to the barn
through the snow
with a bucket of oats
chopped carrots.
his
horse
    turns
as he enters and moves close
a warm gloved hand
                slides
                  along his
pony's side.

the oats are eaten
the carrots crunched
           a wild wind bawls, pushing the wood
the rattle of planks
the solid barn
the howl.

the man and his horse stand quiet.

and down in Cody
the old timers drink their happy hour whiskey
they complain about the weather and shoot the shit
staying out of the cold
away from the snow.

while cowboys stay home
in barns with their ponies
feeding oats
in houses with their wives
feeding lies.
eating pork chops, drinking beer
waiting for the new year and spring
to arrive

and yes
some of those cowboys
most definitely do
love their wives

be he an old timer
or a cowboy

a good man
        does
love his lady

Next chapter

having taken the apartment in Great Falls
the shanty with
the hardwood floors
kerosene
stove and the large plate glass windows
looking out
to the grain silos   beyond

beyond
where I was before

my bedroom painted
a sad sort of blue
like the lonely   grey fields at night

the landlord
seeing nothing, says:
          'paint it
          any color you choose.'

but I
keep it
this sad
sad blue
from where it delivers me comfort
from where I was before.

refridgerator rattle
a ping pong sound
echoes through rooms of lonely
frozen hearts in the night
water
leaks and runs the floor
the rusty pipes *clank, knock, bicker.*

sofa, moved with me
along one wall.
clothes in closets
boots on floors by doors.

seven hundred miles
moving on from every
person I know
this being the call
another
brand new start.
cupboards filled with food and wine
a curtain for the shower
toilet paper, lamp
books, stacked on
the window sill, my
favorites beside my bed.
radio, you too *rattle songs*
from my childhood.
phone in a bucket of water
glasses in a blender of sand and
I take a bite
sitting
naked   on my bed

in
my room
the color
a sad
sad blue

and tomorrow
the same
but adding

the cold
cold cold
grey light

Final days

strip me down to the petty
this is a song I can not sing
broken brush where the ropes
are hidden
tied, tangled, rotting, yet strong
enough to hang a man A. from a
tree or B. a beam where sunlight
has fallen on an empty room
head held high
feel the lonely seep in the air,
across the dirt floors, over the field.
with stink and bogs of rot
which did you choose
where will you die
the burning ropes across your
fingers
your tender neck
cracked
broken
blood now seeping down
dripping
the
green
earth
where you
were
already bound

Iowa Doug

Corn fields of green, sharp, pointed cuts to our
skin. Young and fresh and wanting to explore
we cross the gravel road, down a mile to the
abandoned farmhouse. Up stairs to a tower, a
square door in the floor, we climb, and on top
of the wooden trap we lay, naked, kissing, while

we look out the window to a vast sea of green.
Our cocks in hand we plan our Friday night.
A saddle bag over the garage filled with whiskey,
beer, and Boones Farm wine. To the drive-in, we
flirt with girls, but always in my bed and naked by
two, drunk. Your mother just outside the door.

Young exploration. Sea divers, miners in the mine.
Wild blood needing to know, to experience flesh and
passion. Laughter on tricks of the mind, blind, feeling
our way through to the next day.
But damn, those times were fun. Making love, in cars,
corncribs, wandering, searching unlocked doors.

Every other week

at this kitchen table
looking out this window
to the dull pace of the day
these
weekends
they do grow   lonely   when
my wife has the kids

exwife

I keep forgetting to say

I could drive out   visit Charlie
but he's probably out hunting in the woods
I could go fishing but I don't feel like
that today
could go down to Jim's bar but why
I got cold beer in the fridge and a ball game
that
I   just   don't   feel   like   watching

a couple girls I could call
but they want too much
too close
too soon
so much

grocery shopping on Thursday
the kids
will be back   Friday

that's the only time
this place
comes alive

Nightmare

fire trucks pull to the mountain
smoke fills lungs where no one breathes.
the skies of black, heat, smog, grey,
scorched beyond death in daylight.

someone find Jessica, comfort her as she
screams.

our hearts are broken, for Jessica
the dank ash hill.
this is the place
where Jessica lost her man, her son has
no daddy. the pony absent, burned in the
field. please, please tell the boy, the pony
ran away
please
allow Jessica, to be the one to tell him

the pony *ran away.*

what to tell of daddy, also gone in the field
smoke filled lungs, black, burn, scorched
horrors too real to reveal, in the fields
where daddies die and ponies run away.
the earth left empty, hearts broken
and Jessica, alone, a great deal to carry,
forward with her son in the field.

Silly little slipper

I tried to find a way to love you
coming up from the twisted vine.
Down where the beetles crawl under the skin.
Where Robins and Summer Tanagers must fly and I am always
at your mercy
trying to find a way to get this right.

That is me
        and then
                there is you

with no desire
to see this through.

You drink your gin in the evenings
you play your music,
                you get high
with no need to think of me ever again
too weak to follow your heart or your mind.

Take me with you to the sky
                you beautiful Robins
                    and Summer Tanagers.

And with this cake

46 degrees this morning
and the sun will be gone by noon
on the sidewalk
in front of my apartment
I stand

my friends no longer want to talk to me
they claim I have grown vile and mean
I smile through their confusion
my words
chosen
carefully
to hold them at bay

and then there is that friend
with the heavy eyes and scowling face
he says
I live my life like a
James Frey novel
making it up as I go along
and I swear
with everything I am
I swear
that every bit of it
is true
and if I could hold you just
one more time
he says
I would let every lie go
but you will not call me
he says
so I text you
late in the night
informing you that the knives are
laid out on the counter
come
over

you beg
and finish the job

but I continue to ignore

standing here
staying warm in the sun
my silence
chosen
carefully
to hold you at bay
for while I greatly admire the way
James Frey handles himself
I do not
admire you

I walk back up to my apartment
making a cup of hot tea
and with a knife from the counter
I cut a large slice of cake
you text me to inform me
that you went back on that cruise
and that you slept
with
the most beautiful men in the world
and
I laugh
at your desperation
and then I very tenderly reply
                    yes
                    but what did they
                    sleep with?

I am learning with age
how to be bitter
something I swore I would never be
but why should I give a damn
now

bitter
bitter
when knives
are laid out on the counter
and the sun will be gone by noon

Crucifix

they took the four men
these woman in town
bound and gagged them, drove them up
the hill
dropped them in the dirt
tied them to the trees and hoisted them up

you will pay
they said calmly
Death 2 All Men
your life
ends now
your sins die here
we do not
need
you
we do not want you
die Men
DIE

they cut off their cocks and they boiled their balls
they messed with their heads in the name of justice

but I have done nothing to you
said one of the men

you are a Man
said the Women
you are a Man

Unenthusiastic spectator sport

I tell you clearly the story she told me

"This is the truth!' she said
'Every word, I promise, I swear to God.' she said

'He took me down in the subway.
He raped me down there while people stood
watching
waiting for their train.
I thought people would have stopped him
protected me,
they did not,
they watched.
They were horrified, I could see it in their eyes
they thought it was terrible
they knew it was wrong
but they did nothing to stop him.
I swear they were torn
they wanted to help me
but they watched
start to finish
from the moment he ripped my dress
to the moment he zipped up his pants
and he walked away.'

'What have we become?'
she said with a trembling voice.
'They all stood there and just watched
while he destroyed me
and they did nothing to
stop the
crime
nothing to save me,
to end my pain.'

The worth of badlands

i.

I went back inside to the Native Man who held the bottle of sour mash whiskey. His scar was deep and bleeding. It ran from his cheek down through his heart. His dark eyes filled with pain, his mumbled words ~ sparks of rage.

The Men who had stolen his horse were gone. They were cruel, loud and they were soulless. He moved slow, held out to me the bottle of whiskey. I gestured it for him to keep.

ii.

The sky out here turns darker than the red of rot. Clouds seldom
appear, but when they do they whisp out to the thinnest stories
and they hang far into the dark. Water is only what I carry with
me. Seldom do I find a stream. Not out here, where the Devil
laughs in the wind and that Devil knows my name.

I find a spot in a canyon and make my bed for the night. Wolves
cry far off in the stretch. Bats circle above the warm stone walls
and I wish ~ damn, how I wish that in my hands I held that loud,
cold, mean, bottle of whiskey.

iii.

A pound left of the jerky. Dried blackberries in a folded paper pouch. Soon I must find water. Fill my canteens, water well my horse. She stands tall. She knows this game, this crossing of the badlands she has made this voyage before, and she knows the sound of the Devil at our backs. She too has looked him in the eye.

Cry, cry crazy wolves of the night. Follow close, like the vultures in the sky.

They too lurk for the scent of death.

iv.

The moisture on my body gathers under my hat, on my horse,
her saddle. Another canteen gone dry in the heat ~ from here on
we make our moves through the night.

But for this morning

the sky is cool and clear and we cover many miles. Sparked
wind, cracked skin, the sun burns, blisters through my shirt. The
dry ugly brown, the ground, the hollow sound around us.

We find a patch of scrub brush and we nap through the misery of
the baking afternoon.

I shoot a rabbit, build a fire and pray for a fresh fall of rain.

v.

From a ridge over looking a valley of prehistoric formations of mud and sand, I watch as three men on horses ride down across the worth of badlands. They carry with them a body on another horse, a bound man folded across the saddle. An outlaw heading home for his scathing.

A hangman's noose sounds like relief on this bangled day.
A hangman's noose sounds like heaven.

My horse and I sleep in the shade ~ the time of the sun killing.

The last of the blackberries in the paper pouch.

vi.

The seasons I have passed the badlands ~ over the end ~ close to the name of death. I do not miss this. I wll not challenge more then I do and I do challenge him often. The Devil of this forsaken.

I travel on to a place where she and I will be together. Where I will hold her in my arms. Close is my name when she looks in my eyes and I will not be without her. The dry wind and even my horse whispers her sweetly, and I long to be home beside her.

The worth of the memory, the worth of time. The worth of love held close to the heart. I will reach the green shelter of pine. Across the valley, up the mountain, clean air, birds and ~ butterflies for her hair ~ pulled back and golden, and I will soon be there…

In the dizzy heat as I open my eyes… I see the vultures on the ground around me.

But I pay them no mind as I think of cool water and I think of her ~ touch ~ knowing I will see her in time.

Pistachio ride

Cam, with blue sparkling eyes
a fist full of hair pulled down to the pillow
turquiose and silver shine of light
over this rendezous of flesh and bone

Hotel Monte Vista
     in a room
my ghost splashing water through a phantom kiss
this wish to be a reality
my hands down your rangy hips
carassing legs high to the air
and I take you as mine
sparkling eyes
the kiss of turquoise and silver
time bending and
            far too sweet is this

pistachio ride
     a heart full of passion poured out
         over the pillow

Rubey walk

dreaming of you there on the coast
in the water, floating with the tide
in and out   closer and   further
the   salt   on your skin

the irish whiskey you add to my cup
coffee with fresh whipped cream
and that smile, the rise of your brow
breath-taken   from my body

I miss this and wish you back as
soon as you find your peace
your joy out on   the   water
surfer man of the tide
wishes   in your own heart
dreams float your own mind

sleeping in your truck
by the campfire as the moon
shines   down
wrapped in your blanket
as you are wrapped in my
thoughts
my dreams   of you there
                on the coast

Morning Storm

This morning it was easy to
build a fire
with the snow piled outside
the door, the windows
white glowing in
through the glass
glaring

In a flannel, I stack the wood
the stove still warm from midnight
the faint scent of smoke and charred
pine
socks on my feet
I let the dog outside
I turn and see your picture on
the table

that quick rush ~ of when you were here

Coffee in my mug, I fry eggs, slice toast
sit alone at a table, read the paper while
I eat
I let the dog back in
outside the wind howls
white drifts and powder sparkle by

I dress in boots, heavy coat, hat, gloves
to the barn to feed the horse
the truck snowed under
firewood from the corn crib
I carry a load back to the house
the radio sings that this storm will
last days in to nights
the snow
keeps coming

another cup of coffee

this one with cherry Baileys

                    with a book and my dog
                      we cozy by the fire
                   I drink my coffee and read
                        until I doze
                          I doze
                       off to dream

the wind blasts a wicked howl
branches scratch the windows
sun fades to grey
and then

                          a growl
                  a grunt and a banging at the door
                    a great wild grizzly wants in!
I do not move
                         Quietly
                   I sit on the ceiling and I
                  drink from a jug of wine where
                 turkey sandwiches line along the
                 railing of a bridge over a rushing
            river and apples and daisies fall from the trees
                         and then
                       a shot from
                         a gun
                          and
                  the bear holds my rifle
              he laughs and tells me how it will be
                     and I am wet
                 from the spill of my coffee
                        I wake

still wrapped
in my blanket

                    coffee over my belly
                    my dog sound asleep
                   the fire warm but fading
                   my nap over, my dreams
                          past
                   I open my book and I read

Red Cardinal

Beatrice, stand with the Red Cardinal in the
snow. Watch him, wishing him closer.
Feed him seed as he bounces bare branch
to heaven with your dreams, and Beatrice,
wish him to your daughter who now watches
him moving through the white.

Judy, sit on the mountain, your feet dangling
from the ridge. Hear the song bird
singing for your mother, now gone, she has
flown far away with the Cardinals.
Once returned, sit close, watching as you
wish the Cardinal medicine to your son.

The boy walked through the forest of green pine
buried white in the cold.
In the trees, the flight of red birds
swirling, singing, looking for seed,
where the boy felt the love of his mother, grandmother,
they were there with him in the trees.

More over

Pine covered in white, arctic fox scampers
over snow, where the lynx waits, roams,
searching for a meal in the cold, grey, dawn.
Wolverine, your power, do not run into me.
Wolverine tear your prey, rip, devour, in the
show of sparkling white.

Tracks through the trees of moose and bear.
Caves along creeks where streams babble
through the ice, and flow down to the canyon
making way from the mountain, to other
streams that roll to the Pacific
flowing, fresh water to the salt mix and burn.

Cypress, you goddess of redwood, tallest
in the world. Scale me up with you to the sky
looking out over the earth before man or
the Rockies or the Swiss Alps.
You are Gods: contain a pine martin along
with all of mankind.

Covers

in my bed
overnight and blanketed

in my bed
tracks become edges

in my bed
sparkling and precise

in my bed
freeze on the way over

in my bed
close enough to notice

in my bed
resting like the rain

in my bed
warped in thought

in my bed
wrapped furiously in you

in my bed
upside down in dreams

Whisper the night

he swirled up through the cypress
from the forest floor
this man who loved the green
loved the earth
cast in glory
plaid shirt
strapped boots
sharp axe

we would see him sometimes moving through the wood, his
hands wrapped around that chopper, pipe filled with smoldering
red
through the green ferns that parted as he
walked
along the thicket

he was a god to us kids

a mystery
like Big Foot himself
and sometimes in the early light you would hear a tree fall to the
forest floor, and you would know that it was ~ Big Jake

close
close
getting closer

at night in our tents we would whisper his name and know that
he was watching over
we would tell our stories of seeing him
until we finally would fall asleep
and dream of the lumber jack who was going to save us all

under the mighty cypress that
whispers in the night

On this branch

little wren hops through the branches
his sweet ballad delicate on the wind
his breath a prayer to the
lumber men
who work on in the rain
they build their cozy log cabins
to raise their familes
in
busy
working dawn
till dusk
but always time to stop
and listen for
the
pure
sweet
song
of
the
tiny
wren

Wet

Big Jake on the stump holding his hatchet
hands wet in the rain, bleeding thoughts,
alone in this world he takes my hand.
Ash, pine, tall greens falling down,
the weight of water in his beard,
his face, his sad eyes to mine: tears.

A crown once held high, he understood
the irony, his sharp disposition like the axe
that he grinds, he stands, and chops the trees
until the rains
stop
wait, as all trees die, and he is free

to roam the earth as an axe wielding man
his thoughts not respected, no longer needed.
Big Jake stands on the shores of a cliff and
he dreams and he wishes for a buoyant
tomorrow. Take me with you Big Jake and I will
comfort your soul over the vast, barren mountains.

Strawberry blooms and fish heads

shy little girl with the pigtails
and pigeon-toes had a long w
alk down the lane on her way
to school looking for friends
along the way. Kentucky bac
k roads where the Gulley Gir
ls lived up on the hill and the
Clark Boys caught fish tellin
g lies down by the river. Sec
rets and dates and slipping o
ut of the house while Mothe
r was at work. dropping pea
nuts in cokes and dreaming
of the day they could sail out of Maysville
d

o

w

n

the river 2 Union Town, Port
smith, places, other states w
here dreams were bound 2 co
me true. they wanted husban
ds and houses and   children
and the pigtailed, pigeon-toe
d gal was   jealous of those G
ulley gals, she wanted to be l
ike them. she wanted to be pr
etty like Fay, Jewel, Judy, Su
e, Marie. she wanted to be c
ute like little Tina, she wante
d to date handsome J.B. in h
er frustration she would stan
d on the road above the river
and throw rocks down at the
Clark Boys and they liked it
they weren't picky, they ask
ed her down to the yard, they
pulled her pigtails, told her d
irty jokes, called her sweethe
art so she would stay and pla
y their young boy games

First gear

driving across the mountain in the morning fog
a bottle of whiskey wedged in my lap

cold air trickles through the window.

I drink,
the warm-burning down to my belly to my lap, my legs,
my hands.

I take another, with a swerve and a nod around the bend
and from somewhere in this mist, a thought rolls up,

of you.

> J.B. called to say Cindy is well and will be home
> from the hospital soon.
> I haven't talked to J.B. in years.
> life and time slips through the family even with
> the best intentions at heart.

stopping at the gate, I sit for a few, listening to
Willie Nelson ~ on the radio and, I am lonely in the
green-grey fog
where
deer wander through the field before me.

I snap the switch turning on the heat.

twenty minutes go by.

I open the gate and drive on through, down the highway
into town.

coffee and eggs at the diner where I sit for hours.

the bacon is crisp.

Chapter 20

to the cabin on the river where

                               I fish and wish and dream of
yesterday

when you were here.

I keep photos of you pinned to the wall by the window looking

out to the lake.

where we swam in the summer heat.
your books still line the bookcase. I pick one each week to read.

just having them in bed beside me
gives me comfort.

I read them until I fall asleep.

Paper Willows

still longer at the cabin deciding not to go home.
        lonely here and lonely there
                so I stay in this place with the
        lonely.

on the lake catching fish and letting them go.
        a moose calls out over the valley
                a crow watches me from
          the willow.
        the flowers in the box have died.
I sit on the porch with one of your books unable to concentrate in
                the
                light

        so I wait

        for the night.

thankful another day has ended.

Chapters of night

my soul is starving for something that I can not feed.
a hollow tone that rolls in deep.

moving on means
nothing to me. I do not care. this is all rotting inclination
I must play out with no heart or desire to
make the change that
they tell me will make this wreckage right.

so I stay away from them. they are not here in my thoughts
it is easy for them   to give advice.

and you
where are you now
and do you know that I read your books at night?
and why   did you leave   your books?
please come back to get them   to get me.

the cabin is cold. the fire   has gone out.
I pull another blanket from the bedside and drag it over my head.

a loon calls out on the lake
and I lay here for hours.

I turn on the lamp and read another chapter.

The road to ash

Arkansas
leaving town
back to Santa Fe
you came to get me
filled with promise
that everything would be better in a shiny, genuine
world with a brand new start

two hearts ~ the words
tearful, blue eyes sincere, but broken as you look through.
I thought I loved you

so I went back

and then again
eyes of admiration by another and
a vodka bottle flies past my head
and *shatters the room* - all sanity - *cracked!*
lover's passion left in pieces
true colors, the wild of your brain

insane

the unwarranted RAGE
the clarity
a mistake I made
yet again

two months later

and here I am
back to these adobe walls
fire burning in the kiva
my collar turned high
hot coals
of red
while I
toss the memories
and throw away the pages

ripping then out and over
again
a brand new start

and I forgive
but I
also
burn
with
a *rapid*
rage
a
rapid
rage
I
burn
the
road
I
burn
the road to ash

Spark

I
drop
down with the matches in my hand
a crystal glass ~ filled with gasoline
I look into your eyes
your disdainful words make no sense at all
yet I listen
jagged
sharp
harsh
mean
I sip from the crystal glass that cuts
at my lip and
you cut me deeper
your pain
lost
damaged
broken
and
you take a drink of yourself
I step away with just the thought
of a fire

a new day
I
drop
down
from the city wearing brand new clothes
where coffee in cups are left in the subway
and people smile as they see right through
and there is no warmth in this part of town
where rats run the streets in broad daylight

I look for you
standing far from the fire
you pay no attention

you are lost somewhere inside

in my heavy coat, I walk on

I
drop
down
in a shiny rocket
built just for you and I
the chrome a blast of beauty
the sky a smear of blue
come with me
let us take a ride
closer to the fire
to warmth flowing from the sun
to the mystery of the hollow moon

I
drop
down
waiting until you are ready
my rocket on standby

I
drop
down
I am here
there is no other

I
drop
down
and wait by the fire
inside the burn
the heat of the flame
with a message from
the mightiest man in the moon of glow
come with me
I hear you say

I am that man

Hotel Abilene

red shag carpet walls of green
he was down from Kansas City
    a brown cordaroy coat
    black framed glasses
  hair slicked back with gel
he dropped his
cigarette butts in to his coke
and gazed out over the lawn
            and I just kept asking myself
            why did I take the call
            where is my interest in this

he spoke like a forcaster anouncing
the weather
      on a dark cold day in july
   but it was
     september
       and
   I didn't want to be here
   home alone in bed was my sudden desire

forteen dollars for a roast beef sandwich
we ate as we sat in the lounge
drinking vodka sodas

his room looked out
          over the pool
a lawn chair sitting at the bottom

I took off my coat and sat on the bed

       he promised this was going to be
       some kind of thing but it just felt
       like a waste of time

I felt desperately disconnected from every other human on the
planet
it all felt surreal

I felt stupid, misgiuded and alone

and yet
some part of me wanted to stay

we joined again an hour later
                        back down at the bar

he had showered and changed his shirt and I thought how he
looked a little like Rod Serling and this felt
                        too much like a nightmare
                        episode of the Twilgiht Zone

we sat through a few more vodka tonics
and I hated the taste of his cigarette.

Rest on flowers

I flutter the flame
a courier moth to your beauty.
Your light, the blow of your skills
blurring the fire through the dark I find you
my cock in the wrap of your hand
famous me in, warm bucket of you.

The sweet, sweet nectar of flowers gathered.
Honey enough to keep me alive with more
approach to breath taking closeness, enough to
milk completely, to the chill my skills,
power pull and drain my cock and keep
me an empty caccoon that bleeds.

Take me with you down to Mexico.
The journey we will survive to
nest and make over again to the sun
the cold nights, the bitter bite.
Delicate fine wings of powder
I belong to you and you are mine

The one with no name

Up for air, from the deep of the sheets where we start our affair
of passion. Scrapped limits, where a learned hurricane sucks us
up to the sky ~ on the stage to break again as we keep our
bodies under the ocean for days. And   days   and   days.
Both places are we. Up the airstream and down under the
tide. Ripped. Disheveled. Broken ~ we float ~ we fly.

Recognized hunger within walls of heavy rain.
I speak your name and you pummel me. Again and again.
Where did you come from and where will you go?
Love can only imagine. The distant distraught in your voice and
my mind reels with wonder. Is this real ~ will it last, again
and again ahead of ourselves as we crave this to be of stone.

Begin again, my head full of you. 'Just a little bit, just a little
you say." What? I wonder. "Closer, closer you say, just a little
bit. Just a little." Again we come, wet in the river, our
bodies exhausted. In the dark, still strangers, we share
our wine. We shower separately, dress and go, with only a
number, scribbled on the flesh of a piece of paper.

Chop

Picked of berries the carefully turned lips of
yours speaking chatter under crackled words
of love and fear where balls of snow slam to the
window, fall down melting at the pane.
Swirls of music turn sky grey with heavy
song towards the tranquil barns and cabins.

Flashing through the trees up and over with the
crow who want to fallow directly, they want to
see your face to know your name as I do.
The fox watches from the window this is his
home where he stays warm with me locked
outside running fast through the trees after the

crow trying desperately to keep up. Fox laugh,
fox keep the fire burning. Crow look back and
drop for me crumbs for I am not a fast runner
as you fly. There is no turning back to the cabin
and the fox will not let me inside, and you keep
eating your berries carefully speaking your chatter.

With style

I want to make love to you in New York City.
Pinned down to the concrete while people walk by,
watching us.
Gasping, wondering, wishing, wanting, stepping over.

Let's do this so that everyone sees us, live!
Rip it up, tear me down, show um' all how it's

done.

In the belly of the beast

We were freshly showered,
dressed sharp, and
                    we were
very high.

We hurried to the subway,
fumbled our cards,
we made our way to the open doors of
the train.
I was happy, I wanted to play.
I loved when we shared laughter.
He would try,
but he was uptight.
He would remind me it was work
that the play would come later.
I knew that,
it always did,
we counted on that
our favorite part.
Although he really loved the money.

The roar of the train,
                    so loud.

The passing train,
                    so close.

The crowds of people
waiting to get off.

He reached over,
straightened my cowboy hat and told me that I looked good.
I told him he looked ~ fantastic.

whoosh!

whoosh!

whoosh!

The whirl of the train,
the angry smile,
the lady with bags,   watching.
The creepy man with the glasses, determined to touch me.
I stepped back
with no room to move.

I loved riding the underground train
but only
when we were high.

'We get off at the next one.'
he would say,
and I knew that he was right.
He grew up in this town,
he could get us around,
anywhere,
anytime,
and
he did.

The train would stop, the doors would open and I would
follow him ~ back up to the world above where we would
continue on our way.

EPIC

down the water slides
high on caramel candy
after that great day at
the beach
so
much
laughter
we had never laughed so
much before   not like that

hot showers
back in the cabin and
rest before dinner
cozy, close, curtains drawn
and still
the laughter

that night we sat out on the
balcony, holding hands
listening to music
we watched another
cruise ship
shadow lights in the dark
the tangled romantic
mystery of Cuba

we spoke of all the other
places
in the world we wanted to see
places to go and of our
     dreams
      together
I wanted to paint more and to write
you said you wanted to start yoga
and to slow life down   just a bit more

time
was zooming by, we both agreed

we
watched the dancing of night
out over the Caribbean holding one
another's hand
and then we stepped back into our
sanctuary
turned off the lights, climbed naked
into bed
while watching the silver moon
                        glaze over the Atlantic
the rocking of the ship on the water

and just before
            I fell asleep
you whispered
            into my ear

I love you
            always
                        you said

and we will

        see those places

Time

the warden
called me
a
bastard

I told him
to
go to hell

lately
that son of a bitch
has been pissing a lot of us
inmates
off

teeth grinding
murmers under our breath
lights out
power failure

every
man
has his
fantasy

I see a warden
hanging by a rope

or lock him in with the psychos
or pass him around bunk to bunk
let him know
what it feels like
to be treated with disrespect
a wild
wounded

animal
in a cage
teeth grinding
snarling
spits of rage

there
are
whispers
under the walls
kites passed cell to cell
rumors make their way
and
plans
are laid
when
every man
has
his fantasy

Cell cycle

grey slime of dark red blood

down the cinder block cells

bars of steel cold as hell in

darkness without holy hope

tears fill stainless steel toilets

where orange suits rip in the

wash of gloshing gloom and

muddy ass-wipes over walls

knowing pain, fear, angish,

hate, no room to move, or

hide, or love, for empathy,

grow, or care, or know the

meaning any longer of life

Loving black

"Odd.
You are a little strange."
says mom
"Why I bet when you grow up,
you would even marry a black girl."

"Only if I loved her."
I say, and then,

"No. I wouldn't.
But I would marry a black man."

Mom says nothing.
She goes back to scrubbing her pan.

I go to my bedroom and close the door
going through my record collection I pull out Al Green's
'Have A Good Time'.

The album cover photo is sharp, with Al smoothing back
his hair: warm eyes, flashy smile
and I think,

"Yeah, I'd really like to know this man. I wanna date him, I want
to love him!"

I hit power on my record player, slip out the vinyl, grab my hair
brush and in front of the mirror, I start to sing…

"Smile a little bit more."

Time with Jay

he was pasty
and bloated and his skin was
creepy white
his cheeks were painted rosy

she smirked
and
looked away in disgust
'I hate seeing him that way.'
she said
'Him laying in that casket.'

'Well,
that's what happens when
you die.'
I told her
'That's how you look once they have stuffed you with
embalming fluid and they've patined you with makeup,
bloated and stiff and not real.'

she stood a moment
glaring across the church lawn

'Still,
I haven't see him in years
and I am just saying that he looked awful.'

then she dropped her glasses into
her purse and she walked away.

And the crazy men say

the children run to the school bus
today they will eat a hot meal
toss the guns in the river
drop the pills down the drain
open this padded cell

let me out and I will
tell you
the story

close off the streets
until they are washed
clean
pray
2 your god
4 rain
on this
sunny day that goes on forever

Shattered exhaust

I stood outside your window
and I watched and waited and

YES
I am the one who threw the rock
I am the one who broke the glass
the shatter, the crash ~ that woke you

and yes
          I did just admit to it
          proud to own up to that

the rock, was warm in my hand
I clung tight when I held it and I flung it
HARD and I
smiled as it flew

a WHIZ and a WHOOSH through the air
          then
          the *crash*
          the *smash*
          of glass
     the satisfation!

bits of sharp ice that scattered your floor.
shards scraping and dragging under your front door.
bits of bite to your feet each time you step.

am I evil

in my confession that I slept well
that night?

I don't care if you call me malicious
call me anything you like
we have both seen better days.

Now, YOU confess the break you broke on me.
it is your turn sweetest of hearts…
You confess…

the turn you tore

the bullets you shot

the bang of the head

the stab of the heart

the drain of the blood

the lies to the mind

the shock to the system

Step Up

Come clean to

the bomb you dropped on me

the rage of hate and anger

the claim you swore from love

the pages you wrote in rage

the tangled rope

the smoke of lies

the canon to the soul

THE BREAK
        YOU
    BROKE
    ON ME

Toy cars in sandy pits

So what if I woke this morning, eyes opened, sad inside.
Death lurks around the corner stepping up in the morning light.
I shake it off while I wish it were over
waiting for the coffee to work it's way in deep.
Where I start again to care, to think of ways to make it
through, to make it better, make it right.
Caught up in the distractions of the day, the constant work
of survival. The hours, the days, the weeks, the months, the
years.
I drive my toy cars off of cliffs into sandy pits that on
rainy days fill with water. Then the little me is trapped in
the little cars and the little me drowns and in panic I feel
the fear until I wake again in the morning.

Speed

Behind the wheel of his Tesla
he drives through the badlands of New Mexico.
Black lava rock, white sands, enclose him
while love blooms in his heart. His cock
hard, he thinks about her, wanting her lips on
his; time and passion, they will come.

Batteries charged, wheels burn the pavement
wind in his hair, music bangs his box.
He thinks of her and wants her body on his.
He wants her naked always, always, always,
he wants her beside him in his car
and the time will come, she will come, he will come.

At a stop along the road, an empty gas station
burger and fries and watered down coke.
Past the lava rock, white sands, his cock hard,
he gains speed while he thinks of her legs,
her arms, her box coming, his cock coming.
He speeds up knowing, the time will come.

On the outside

you are so fine, gorgeous!
he said

yeah, sure
she said
in this light
in the dim of this bar
both of us drinking
of course I look good
cute
pretty
gorgeous
you might even say
go on
say it
go on
say it
go on tell me

I said it
he said
I will say it again
you are fine
gorgeous!
GORGEOUS!
GORGEOUS!
I wish you were mine!

she smiled and took a drink of her wine

then
take me home
I will go with you
strip me down in your bed
spin me around all night
you already thrill me with your smile

                          put your talented hands on my body
                            make me believe in magic
                              we both will be happy
                                  this I know
                               thrills in the night
                                   take me
                                   show me
                                   make love
         however

                                 in the morning
                               when you roll over
                           you will not want to see me
                                 and this I know
                                from experience
                                      you
                                   will not
                                  look at me
                           will not look me in the eye
                                   you will
                              grumble in the sheets
                                turn your head
                        you will drag your dick to the toilet
                               rush to the kitchen
                             wishing with each step
                                   that I go

he smiled and took a drink of his beer
oh,
I get it
he said
this is your way of brushing me off
trying to chase me away
you don't want to be loved
you think all men are shallow
only interested in a
one night fuck
well,
not all
there are lessons in life

time will teach
that many of us men
we do love
to
love

                                                      no
                                                she said
                              this has nothing to do with love
                        I am truly only beautiful by the light of
                                                the moon
                        I have seen myself in the sunlight and
                              no one wants to be seen that way

                    the moon
                    the moon
                    is my
                    savior

I know the curse of life
he said and then added
I know the beauty by the
light of the moon
I hunger in the magic of night
                        and he smiled at her
                          she smiled at him
                        they went home together
                        he stripped her down in
                                his bed
                          they made wild
                                crazy
                          wonderful love
                        moonlight through
                            the window
                          gasping for air
                            whispers of
                              passion
                        he spoke of her beauty
                          she spoke of his
                              moonlight
                              moonlight
                        through the window

                              98

and in the morning
golden sunlight past the curtians
golden sunlight through the
glass

she woke before he did
she sat up
her reflection in the mirror
hair in her face
she leaned over
and watched him sleep

in her eyes
he was just as beautiful
as he was the night before
she wondered what dreams
were swimming in his head
she wondered what he
thought of her
she
stayed watching
until

he started to wake
she
panicked
she slipped out of bed
pulled on her dress
picked up her shoes
and she quietly
so
quietly
walked out the door

they never spoke
again

cycle break

I
think of the sex
I shared with you
while I lay alone
in my bed
the sheets
still
wrinkled
sheets
we shared
not yet washed
sex
with you
never again
this room with you
never again
alone here
in my bed
these
dirty
sheets
and I will wake in the morning
with hope for the new day
I will set out with new meaning
but
by the end of noon
I will be
broken
alone
here in my bed
these sheets
my dark room
as night falls
and it all turns
again

Rita's holy ground

she drove to the farmhouse
with one small bag

she turned up the drive
she turned off her phone

by the light of the fading sun she
unlocked the front door

she sat on the livingroom carpet
and cried

night fell
she stayed in the dark

she stood at the window
her mind numb, rolling over

the rhubarb patch
thinking of her prize winning pies

she walked up stairs
laid on her bed

pulled a blanket over her
and cried

she misses her daughter
married now, living in New York

her son the doctor
ear, nose and throut

so busy
too busy

to call
'but I love you mom'

her husband
the cold handed bastard

his demands
his screams

'he takes me for granted'
she hates him and she loves him

she goes down stairs
boils water for tea

and with
the blanket

she sits on the porch
behind the screen

through the darkness she sees
the barn

the rusty tractor
memories of her mother, her dad

the many years they have been gone
she thinks of lost chances

her time at college
thoughts of her book club

the women she somehow knows
without saying
feel the same inside

she could smell the green
drifting from the wild weed patch
where a thriving garden once stood

a cold air drfting in around her
the clock ticking in the hall

time spinning forward and back

dreams and memories

lost and found

she drank her tea and went back

inside

and cried

Warning label

 and I warn you
 if I can not
 take this any
 longer
 if I am unable
 2 bare

WHAT will you think of me?
as you say, do not say that, do not speak of death
but I will say what is where my mind wanders in
this late of life that I care

let us not pretend any longer that we ALL don't feel this at times
if I only keep my smile for you 2 see, then you will claim
I am not honest, claim me 2 be insincere

 so I warn you
 if I can not
 take this
 any longer
 if I are unable
 2 bare

do not think you have the answers, hate me if it helps you 2
feel you are in control of your can not be

WHAT will they think of YOU?
If you decide 2 show your face for real and you dare 2 say 2
them
if you warn them

if you can not
take this any
longer
if you are unable
2 bare

Shotgun

floating between my legs are my memories
of you.
drowning heart in a flood of take me down again
I miss you and I wish you were here.

with a six pack of beer I drive to the river.
with a shot gun in the truck I dream of ending it all.
but no. I crack a can and swallow down the anguish
cold beer burning, sucking my
soul.

and you, already with another. someone we both knew.
I question your love as I watch the river. I grab a can and
open another.

floating between my legs are my memories of you.
I want you here in this truck beside me.
not the gun
not the heartbreak
you
already in the arms of another.

another can I toss in the river - watching it float with the
current to hell.

I strip down and step in the water
the cold floating between my legs
my heart beats faster
while broken

I miss you and I wish you were here.

I miss you and I wish you were here.

little fish

there was a fire
           at the lake
and the firemen called out my name
           but I was not there to answer
              I was already down
        down
          at the bottom of the cold grey
        fish
         down
            under the wet sheets of ash

down
   in the darkness
  gone
before the fire
before they

        ever

          missed

  me

and I am happiest here beneath the water
                 happiest stuck in mud

lost

soon forgotten

my mind resting with not a care in the world with only one hope

that they never find my body.

PJ

She waddles to the bar with an angry face
her hair shaggy, scarf tight around her neck.
She chokes on her anger and her anger rides
her deep, rides her hard, owns her mind.

Hey PJ, waddle to a booth and drink your beer,
talk about all the woman you hate.

Says PJ, 'I leave every job where there is
a woman. I hate all women.' she says,
'I can not get along.'

She sits in a booth and looks out the window.
Playing pinball she swears at the machine.
Three beers in a row and two cocktails, she
grows loud, angry and mean.

She is a trickster who will turn truth around,
play the friend while inside it is you she hates.
Contempt for women, hell, contempt for men!
She waddles to the bar for three beers in a row.
Shaggy, shaggy, filled with rage, shaggy, shaggy,
filled with hate.

Waddle, waddle, PJ, to the bar, waddle, waddle
do your hate.

Shades

the woman in yellow stepped to the
edge of what?
where she claimed she could see forever
what she looked at she would not speak of
what she reflected was all we could know
and we loved her
we wanted her and dreamed in our hearts

the shades murmur
in the wind
someone pull down the shades

on this dry windy day where the air rushes
the tongue
where the large-flowered cactus bites the
Prickly Pear
the Rebutia drinks the Blue Myrtle
Eve's Pin and Saguaro at the top of the hill
they bind in dreams ~ as they chew Peyote

and the woman in yellow steps over this land
careful not to harm
the woman in yellow speaks of loves desperation
that she claims to see so clearly
and you love her

the shades murmur
shades rattle
shades crack
I pull down the shades

and I leave this house where the rocks tumble the
mountainside and water floods the plains as the
ledgend is told
it is a lie

it is the story
the only water is the salt of the sea
fresh dew trickles down leaves at night to
mouths that are open to tongues that cry
but this means nothing to Eve's Pin or
to Blue Mytal who have all that they need
salvation and tears of the soul
desperation
small drops they hold inside

the woman in yellow steps to the edge of
what, where she claims to see forever
and the rest of us listen while we ask
'*see what?*'
and we want her and need her and love her
so we see

still the dry desert air drifts in under the clouds
that no longer cry
it is sand and dust that line the walls and bury
the window sills deep
where
the shades murmur
the shades crack
with wounding regret
you pull down the shades
forever

When today

She held my hand as we left breakfast
she had cried the night before
she wasn't happy and I knew

back at the motel she started packing
talking about a man from work
I don't really remember all of that part
I couldn't allow myself to hear

she deserves to be happy
and so do I
we would be better apart

      I suddenly remember a day years ago
      a smile she held and her laughter
      fresh face   she always found me funny
      always   I could make her laugh
      now we both ran dry
      the green had gone leaving a sadness
                      a desperation

this will be good for us both
a new start with respect for the past
I took her hand   looked her in the eye and smiled

we drove back down the mountain listening to one of her
audio books about a lonely man in a haunted house in the city

In the patch

The berries rot here in this basket
they turn, wither in the bowl,
over gains they will never share,
over consumption they will never know.
Berries decay without fever
as human flesh with fever decays.

She steps out to the briar patch.
Her dress torn by the thorn, her skin
bleeds, she is hungry, but the berries
are soaked with the eggs of the insect,
the sky rains acid and she can not see
still, she picks the berries.

'I am hungry, I am hungry.' she says.

She looks through the cupboards quickly, moving,
food there in the pantry. She eats her grain, without
the berry, she chews what she can not see.
Over her consumption they will never know,
she moves down through the cutting briar
as she longs to eat every last berry.

Fleeting

burning timbers tumble from the air to the side of
the table where you drink your wine and
you
do not want to go
you want to stay through the tragedy

'Go?'
you say, "Go where?

Why should we worry, what good will that do?
Why must we be the ones to sacrifice?

the sirens howl
'Evacuation! Time to leave. You must go!'

your steak is set on the table before you,
bringing a smile to your face

'Let the earth crumble.' you say

slipping your plane ticket back into your bag
you continiue on with your wine and your steak.

deciding on your comfort
in these last days.

End of the complex

they have cleared this block
trampled flowers, chopped down trees
houses have been burned
locks were picked, valuables taken
there are no cars left in the drive
no mail man to deliver
no mail
smoke over the mountains
babies cry at night
sirens from the other side of town
a man screams
'It's the end of the world!'
with no one around to listen
just you
and
you
watch this all happen
from the safety of
your window
you close the curtains
like turning off the tv
they are dying, but this is not your concern
they need water
food, medicine
'I am not feeling well.'
you say
and so you lay down
in your bed
and you
sleep
slipping your head
far under the pillow

Time to go

there were so many of them
hundreds and hundreds
tens of thousands!

the streets were crowded
as far as you could see
they came over the hills
across the bridge
down over the houses
they were
everywhere
and they kept coming faster
and faster
it was insanity
it was unbelieveable
they dropped from the trees
they fell from the sky
it was a nightmare
it was a horror
it was crazy
it was

a relief

damn it all to hell!

it was hard to admit

it
was a relief

Clock

running down the street I call to the cabs on the corner

not one stopping or slowing or caring

I walk home

pigeons follow me along the electric lines and the rain cinders

fall endlessly with season, my shoes black, once as white

as snow, once clean with miles to wander

I step quickly past the crowds on the corner, searching, asking

for the time of day

no time they tell

no time I say

and I keep on walking through the embers

through the end of day

past the running

blood

in the streets

The usual reality

coming down from the north
where the ships had landed
we carried our food and water
to the abandoned house
hidden by trees
she
spoke Italian
there was fear in her eyes
she set us up in a room with a bed
then left us alone
others were in other rooms
they too had seen the ships
they too, forced to believe
'They
will
save
us.
They have been here all along.'
we heard a man saying out on the lawn
'they have been guiding us
our only saviors.'

we undressed and crawled into bed
we held one another close and
we slept with dreams of
aliens

the next morning we were on our way
on down the valley
to the only parts that remain
where the fires had not burnt
where the floods had not washed
and the earthquakes left some
people standing
earth, sky, and sea.

You are home

the hills are lined with little houses, that are pink
and green and yellow. woman in striped pants smoke
and laugh and call out to the men who walk home from
their day in the city where they buried their hearts
lost their souls to the dust and grime

the houses on the hills will be there for years
people will come and go
they die and their bodies are buried
                                on the other side of town

in the cemetary
                with everyone they do not know

but their hearts and souls live on in the deep mines of the city,
the air, the dust and the grime
little houses on hills
                pink, green and yellow

SAVE US!
you scream
as
you run down the street
in every color

Climate range

and you do know

the words

rivers breaking damns

taking houses to the sea

the shifting of the

planet

the melting of ice

dripping

sloshing gallons of endless

water

cars under currents

houses floating by

we

made our way up

the hill to the church where we sat on the step watching

my wife

cried tears

for our loss

but

we

were thankful

to be alive

shifting life as the planet relocates all

to the constant

rapid

ravage

towards survival

the continued

realization

of

change

Protest Last - take a number

do you not see the insects are dying
there are so few birds these days
where our hearts bleed on the pavement
as you complain of such nonsense
and waste your time
damn
this ship
     that sinks
this ship
      caught in the whirlpool the
mugging tide

FUCK these pointless dreams
this candy coated world we are trained to lust for
FLASH
&
MONEY
&
you believe there is solace in great wealth
FUCK
the well sheep, FUCK, the wall. FUCK the plastic cards we all
slide on ~ down.

would you call this the end of time
do you think it will all be over soon
do you wish it to be
would you rather it go on forever
artic melt where the birds are buried
trees dead under what we wish in green
water poisoned in lead
plastics melt our minds

and we go on as if there is nothing
we go on in our dreams to live forever

ask4angles

through the dust where the wind roars the valley
over fields and cities of fires burning
sun muddles through the vail
and here we
stand
starting over on top of this hill

MOUNTAINS
rain and rivers roaring running
green we pray and beg for
berries and melons and corn
to feed our needs
our bodies
our souls
broken
ravaged

so many gone
starting over
rolling down
canyons
filled

with
H2O
printed on
plastic bottles
uP
from the
mud
after
the storm

more
STORMS
N FORECAST

Dance Nightingale

Dance Nightingale is from another world.
He is sharp and intimidating.
A man one finds it hard to look away from.
He wears a full plush hat of red velvet.
Rose petals flutter
down
from
the
sky.
They scatter
over him
as he sits in a chair in a long, lanky fashion,
like a spider
constantly weaving his web.
He is a dream maker.
His lap covered in a sea of long stemmed roses
he takes them in his hand and drops them at his side.
His lips burn red
a heavy brow
he speaks with the voice of a God.
A roll of thunder and rain moving over the land
commanding.
A life force that captivates,
you are seeing something you are not meant to see.

Yes
I want to know you, Dance Nightingale.
You
are
 a
dramatic
masterpiece.

The salvation of Dance Nightingale

the nightingale
the nightingale
the nightingale knows
dance dance dance
Dance Nightingale

and from this world
I watch you
from this space
I see it all
look at me

you are not getting away unnoticed
do I say it again?
look
at
me

Dance Nightingale
I have earned that name
Dance
Nightingale
the nightingale knows
through the wisdom and growth
of a life time of years
reaping the rapture of love and the devine
paying the price of mistakes and fear
living in the dark and the light

it is not like you think
your fluffy white clouds that you sit upon
your clean little hear after
that you think you have the answers too
how arrogant you are

we all choose what we believe
what choice did you make?

dance dance dance
Dance Nightingale knows
fear the dark and the light
you find your reasons to love
you find your reasons to hate
which do you do more
love or hate?
love
or hate?

you know nothing but what man has guessed
                              dance
                              dance
                              dance
                    Dance Nightingale

you do it all again, I will tell you that
they took that part out
it did not serve them
to their power over you
but you do live your life over and over
until you learn what you need to learn

colors?
you have been them all
judgements?
you have made them all
you are so much more then you see

mistakes?
revel in them!
for they are here and now
they are everything
your blueprint that shows your structure
your cast that bears your soul

love?
you run!
you close your heart and you learn not to
for you learn that it is all there is
that it is the only reason to be
the reason you exist

and still you run
you close your hearts
blind fools
you waste your time here
broken and fearful hearts

       in the pine and the dill and the caraway
       the orange blossoms and red clover
       I would take your soul
       I want your soul

       in the orange blossoms and red clover

life is learning to keep your heart open
thats all it is
love or fear
your heart
open or closed

roses anyone?
the thorn on the stem
we prick ourselves as we make our way
to the breathtaking core
the purest light
the bright colored sweet scented
heart racing glow
the nectar we long to taste
and dream of in the night
the desperate longing

we prick ourselves over and over and over again
for that taste we dream
we long for flesh
to comfort our heart
to satisfy desire

rest your mind
       I will sooth your soul
       to a passive role
       and gently wind you over

your world or my world?

Dance Nightingale can see it all from here
you hear my words and I see your face
but only for this moment in time
here my words with an open mind
and know that I see much deeper

drop a quarter in a shot glass and fill it with patron
                swallow the silver coin
                    smooth in your gut
                        feel it and tell me
                        is it heads or tails?

what would you do for love?
what have you done for love?
oh the stories you must have there
we wreck ourselves for love
and come up blaming the other

                *I slam my fist on the table with a
                        mighty* BANG!

and I look at you
while you refuse to see me
                        dance dance
                        Dance Nightingale

I watch the sky above
while rose petals fall from the heavens caressing my face
alone in my chair
with a furrowed brow
the rose petals fall soft on my skin

we all came here tonight with walls and masks
just so we all step up and admit it
that you are doing this everywhere you go
building walls
wearing masks

in your gut

in your quiet time alone
admit that you are doing this
that most of the time
your heart is closed
and that you wear your masks and build your walls
that you like it that way because *it makes you feel safe*
because you know fear
and you allow fear to win

break down the walls
break down the fear

the dog tags around your neck
what do the dog tags read?
read me
tell me
what the dog tags say
how would you best describe yourself in few simple words?
                    my dog tags read:
                        painter
                        cowboy
                    passionate man!
                     great desire
                   love and beauty
                     velvet ropes
              rose petals on a cowboy bed
                      stay close
                  in my cowboy arms

in this light
dance dance dance
Dance Nightingale

I wanted that moment with you and I had it
that cherished and beautiful moment with you by my side
close
in this light

we have all done things for love and passion
we all know where our desires our secrets
take our hearts in the middle of the night
desire

long for

we spend our lives yearning
dreaming
wanting
searching
for a power we are terrified of
surrender your power
love and desire

dance
dance
Dance Nightingale

but you are not ready
please stop acting like you are
stop pretending you know it all
stop and look and see
open

let me tell you of a lifetime of love
let me speak of my heart
then I shall leave you alone
alone to reflect
on your own way of love
love lost
love held
love left behind
hearts that you have damanged

I loved you the moment I saw you

or I must say at the very least I was darkly captivated
your beauty was like this rose
fresh with perfection and I could not walk away
a slow burn that sparked in my brain
a fire that ignited my chest
my flesh was seared
damned was my soul
devotion and desire
I wanted you

then

when you wanted me
when you took to my bed
and you moved in close
and you said you needed what I had to give

I was born anew
holding you in my arms
took my breath away
and I helped you
ravage my heart

you came to me
you needed me
in your tears you cried my name
you said you wanted me and *I liked that*

a fist full of roses I toss in the air
                                passionate
                        I thunder in my chair!
wanting to leave
wanting to come find you
                scattering roses and desire *everywhere*

yet in the morning light
you could not handle what the night had so easily given
and my heart sank oh mighty sailor
it sank in the sea of whiskey
that then became my best friend
and yours
you needed the whiskey as well
the one friend who could please us both
and we both let-him-in
take me under   warm glass of you and I

and then we moved on
from the burn that was mutually disgarded for the
understanding spirit and nectar of the blue agave
the heart of the pineapple
the heart of the blue the only heart we could share

that clear alixir that calmed our desperate nerve

that covered our pain and disappointment

and like my dynamite father before me
I hid the pain and buried my soul
in the back yard
under the tree we named patron
that might oak
and again you crawled in to my bed
again and again I thought there may be something to save
a love that would satisy and
it
did

until
the burn stopped somewhere in the night
sober in the darkness the cold fearful dark
the green-grey of early dawn
when you once again only knew my name
and passion was back in the ground
in the yard
under the tree

the emply bottle
as hours passed
the dawn
the days
the dark
the drink fading to light
the love and devotion evaporated from memory
like dreams that never happened
sweet dreams
I try not to forget

you are not ready

PLEASE stop acting like you are
as I love in my *crazy passion*
nothing less

stop acting like you are

then my prayers led me to salvation
attachments to hope

            salvation of a cowboy man
    a tattooed maverick and his cowboy love songs
            these are the words that I am

the wirl of wind
and the universe handed me a great responsibility
a lesson to learn now or in the future
so I chose now
sorting through my fears and devotions

                    my rage of passion softens
                    the golden sun light shines
                    a blue cast as it starts raining
                    and I step back into the night

that cleansing rain to snow through the open window
to the pine trees outside   where
three bull elk
strolling and grazing the fresh white
looking for spring grass on the forest floor
and
for one hour of my life
in that early silver light
the quiet
the perfect drops ~ heaven falling...

                ...I held you close to me while you slept
                    your warm skin pure and soft
                like the white drifts outside the window

and there are other memories
so many   sweet   tender   memories and so
from this world
I watch you
as the finale walk plays out

we have all been loved and lost
reached out and been rejected
these are life's lessons
we must go through
our attachments, our fears
our desires, our loves

salvation

salvation

where the rose petals fall
where the roses run wild
that sharp and beautiful pain
your roses
white lilies
peonies of the kind
they burn the wild raging heart
the brutal
broken
soul

the desperate
mangled
mind

the shattered
spirit

part two

If you are not going to laugh
then stay away from me all weekend

and please put your panties back on.

He said, "This is California.
I can do whatever the fuck I want."

Valley of Fires

1981

Edith Head has a show downtown so I
take the bus to buy my ticket.
she is ill this day and I miss her.

at Otis, I study costume design
not yet the painter.
in all of my classes I make friends.
still, I only let them so close.
on the weekends a bus to West Hollywood.
this young man who studies and takes it all
in and I learn
                quickly
and I quickly grow up.
there is no going back to the farm in Iowa,
in Missiouri I will never live again.

Los Angeles, you are excting, and now
you are my home.

the palms along Wilshire
summer days at Venice Beach
Hollywood & Vine
bright night clubs, a world of mixed cultures.
I drink
White Russians.
at 19
here
my heart will settle
learning of   love
              and
              sex
              and
              life.

Studio 1

we dance to Billy Idol
Sylvester, Culture Club, Grace Jones
sings ~ *Pull up to the bumper, baby!*

Girls on Film and 96 tears
Laura Branigan, Prince, Annie Lennox
George Michael, Soft Cell.

we run the streets filled with life
Hollywood, Silver Lake, to Long Beach
back to L.A.
we dance
club 2 club every weekend,
the Pink Elephant on Thursday nights
just to dance
Louis with his afro
GiGi with her curls
dress up
go out
drink
and dance
sweat
laugh
then to Ships Diner to sober up
and laugh
home by dawn watching MTV
this new chick named Madonna

a few hours sleep
           before we lay in the sun by the pool
           and rest
           gearing up
           for the next night
of wild dancing
under the L.A. stars!

Budding actress

in a bungalow in Hollywood
pointsettia trees outside the window
I help her study her lines
scene by scene.
she is
going to be
a movie star!

there is a spark of light in her soul
a talent for seeing magic in her approach.

this reading, for a part in a movie
a call back, so she has a good chance.
she gives it her all
with her bright blue eyes she cries
when the page instructs.
she makes you feel it all so real.
she is an actress.

we read through it several more times
then stop to make a sandwich.

there is a love scene on page 40
and when I see her grow weary
I tell her we must practice
that.

her smile is magic and her dreams will
come true.
her desires to be up there on that silver
screen in bright golden light.

her love scene alone
deserves an Oscar.

The crush

it was a Wednesday night not a Friday night
you called.

do you have champange

yes

may I come over and may we have a glass, I have something
I am burning to tell you.

so on a Wednesday night not a Friday night you came.
we drank a glass of the bubbly
then you stammered and laughed, you took your time but
finally told me what you had come to say.

that *you loved me*
that you had for the past two years.

and then
you waited
for my response

and what could I say

I told you, I love you
as a friend
that you mean
the world to me

my friend.

You grew quiet and told me to forget every
word you had just uttered
forget eveything you just said

but how could I

out there in the air

both knowing how one another feels
let us move forward with the friendship
all is okay.

but you could not
and you grew bitter
then your anger that I would not be as you dreamed

and you grew distant and mean
until you hated me
and would not speak to me a word

Wednesday nights and Friday nights and weekends came
and went
and we never
laughed, shared champagne or our friendship again.

and for always
I missed you

Celebrity tours

this is the spot where Woody Allen filmed
Annie Hall,
although everything has changed.
that was once Sonny Bono's restaurant.
this is Spagos at the Hotel Bel Air, and this is
Ryan Goslings place, boy is the food
ever good!

this is Robert De Niro's Nobu, he has one in
Malibu too, but we
                    will be
having hot dogs for
lunch today
at Pinks.
this street was in the movie, China Town, and this
one in the BIG Lubowski.
in that building there, lived Bette Davis.
this building here was in The Long Goodbye.
don't you miss Robert Altman?

this Benedict Canyon home was once owned by Eddie Murphy,
built by Cher.
I don't know who lives there now. Most likely an attorney.

Kirsty Alley lives here, Marilyn Monroe lived there, and
somewhere behind these walls lives Drake.

I met Steve Martin here one day, he was the perfect gentleman.
Tatum O'Neil was a total bitch! I met Jaclyn Smith at the Rite
Aid in Beverly Hills and the next day I met Farrah Fawcett, that
was years ago. she was with Ryan O'Neil and he was not a
happy camper.
Jaclyn Smith and Farrah Fawcett, truly were angels.

this is a Frank Lloyd Wright house, a wonderful work of art!

now we are driving down Mulholland Drive where Mulholland
Drive was filmed.
this is Hollywood Blvd. and up there is the Hollywood sign.

this is the freeway from La La Land.
did you know that most movies were once filmed in L.A.?

Robert Downey Jr. lives in that house, there is a guy always
going through his trash.
Sam Mendes lives... right... here!

Leonardo Decaprio is selling that place, some times he is out
there and he waves.
Right here they filmed the movie Night Crawler, and over there
Jackie Brown.

this house belongs to Adrian Gonzales, is that not a beautiful
house?
Batman was filmed here.
Did you see the movie Magnolia? Willam H. Macy is always
here in Beverly Hills.
Julian Moore shops in Beverly Hills, Gwyneth Paltrow shops in
Beverly Hills and once I saw Rhianna.
Hell, they all
shop
in Beverly Hills.
That building there was once Bonwit Teller and the Brown
Derby was there.
but
those golden days
are gone.
be sure to watch L.A. Confidential for the feel of old Hollywood
and while you are at it watch Barton Fink and Singing in the
Rain.

OH LOOK!
There is Kristen Stewart!
Oh wait, she just *looks* like her.

Don't worry, *we will see stars!*
if we just keep driving. but next we are heading to the Getty
Museum, then to the Santa Monica Pier, and then to Malibu, to
see... Cher's beautiful castle home.
Maybe *she will invite us in!* She is cool that way

Lebanese man

your olive skin, body covered in fur,
on your bright beach towel
looking out to the ocean.
you watch the swimmers in the mass,
colored trunks around their necks
bobbing the Pacific,
slim beach bodies in coppertone,
coconut oil, and sunglasses.
a cooler of coke, your audio book,
you
ride your bike to this beach,
everyday,
Lebanese man.

to the Venice boardwalk to buy a hot dog and
yogurt, where you wander through the
crowd, then back to your towel,
where you sit again and gaze
out to the water.

you think of nights before.
you dream of nights to come
in your apartment in Marina Del Rey.
no view of the ocean there,
but a space that is all your own,
until someday, when your dreams move you
forward
and out of L.A.
beautiful,
Lebanese man.

Finding Sean Penn

Mike tossed his cigarette into the gutter
he stood, looking at the sign.
I am going to do this.
he said,
tonight.

Don't be a fool.
she said,
Do you know how much these things cost?
I mean the ones like you want to get.
Those little silly ones,
those don't cost much,
but what you want
those cost money.

Those little silly ones are for pansies.
he said,
People afraid of making a statement.
Does it hurt?
I am so worried it't gonna hurt.
Better give me a little moon or
a star.
Those are the light weights who get those
little tweety birds or tiny flowers,
or baby mushrooms ~ what-the-fuckever.
I am not afraid,
and I am more then ready to make a statement.
I want the entirety of my back to be
one big-ass picture of Taylor Swift.

I swear to God!
she said,

I do not
get that!
You don't even listen to her music.

Don't care.
he said,
I think she is one fine looking piece-of-ass!

What about me?
I am just as pretty as Taylor Swift
and
you actually know me
you actually get to fuck me.

Yeah, but
how do you know that while I am fucking you
I'm not thinking about Taylor Swift?

Oh really?
Wow
well
you had better not be, dickwad.
And for your information,
since you wanna be all honest about this shit,
I often imagine
while you are fucking me,
that you
are Sean Penn.
And I mean I imagine that a lot!

Sean Penn,
what the hell?
That dude's old enough to be your dad.

I don't give a shit.
He's not my dad,
and he happens to be crazy hot and crazy interesting.
And damn it, but I do wish you were him.

Fucking A.

Nice.
Real nice.
Thanks for telling me that.

you might need to realize something here.

What?

If I were Sean Penn, I wouldn't be fucking you.
I would be fucking Taylor Swift.

Super asshole you are.
Go get your bad-ass tattoo.
I hope it bleeds, festers and burns.
You
are gonna look like an idiot with Taylor Swift on your back.
But goddamn it,
I know I am gonna look damn fine with Sean Penn on mine.

Workers

they chased us back today
out of the fields of California.

'Go back to Mexico!'
someone shouted.

there was a gun shot
but no one ran
we stood there
in the hot sun in straw hats
waiting
watching the men in the truck
the woman in her fancy car
who cursed our children
in that cabbage field we
had been working for weeks.
in this place we wanted to be
but were not welcome.

they do want their vegetables on their
tables, they do want their yards green.

we were sent home for the day
back to Mecca.
we made a meal, played music
and sang.

tomorrow
we return to the fields.

Josh

I concider it a good sign I found your number on the
bathroom wall.
it tells me a lot about you.

if you wrote the number there yourself,
you are confident and outgoing.
you believe in who you are, possessing little fear.
you like to meet new people,
you like adventure, you are clearly not a snob.

if you are not the one who wrote it,
it tells me you are popular in a crazy sort of way.
clearly not boring, you are on people's minds.
either way, much loved for your talent of giving head
or
someone is very jealous of you and you are very much
despised.
which also indicates you are in someway or another
outstanding.

I scribbled your number on my arm.
I'll call you and we'll take a ride.

Self-delivery

I brew a hot cup of black tea
place the chinese food container N the
microwave.
cut a fresh slice of ginger
and open the plastic cup of hot mustard

I am slopping around 4 a 10AM breakfast.

        with a horrible headache last night
        one so bad I could not lay down
        pacing the floor back and forth
        until the
        medication kicked in

   cloudy this morning
   damn it, but thanks 4 that
   no sun and a clear-shot-view of the freeway

a catch of my eye and
damn it again ~ but somehow there is mustard
down the front of my robe

fuck it
      sitting in my chair at the table

I take a bite of ginger and enjoy the burn with a swallow of beer

        lemon chicken
        the perfect breakfast
    when you don't have the taste 4 eggs and
    you didn't eat dinner last night

going from beer 2 tea
back and forth
gazing off down the freeway
I open a fortune cookie
it reads:

Listen these next few days to your friends to
get answers you seek.

I dont like the sound of this advice. If I had the right friends
I wouldn't be eating alone.

I open a bottle of asprin. slam 3 of them in my mouth.

another sip of tea, another swig of beer.
I open another fortune cookie.
it reads:

You will have a close encounter of a surprising kind.

Perfect!
now this is a fortune I want to believe
one I am eager 2 see come true.
damn it all 2 hell ~ but I need a little good luck.

I enjoy the rest of my tea and cookies
place the dishes N the sink
pull on my shoes and coat
and set out 2 the city
                    N search of
                    and willing
4 my close encounter to begin.

oh, and my lucky numbers are:

20   22   23   24   48

California Soul

1.

we were down on the beach when the wave came, surfers
wall to mighty wet wall.
it was rad, man, *ripped* and *roaring!*

Lisa was sucking on a snow cone
from snow she gathered up in Tahoe and carried down through
the rain.
singing Joni Mitchell, naked, on the hood of her car.
the bitch was solid, loud, she was mean.

that's when the earthquake, man! came rolling through the
valley.
buildings
falling
to
the
streets.
fuck
rock
& roll
people running to the top of the Hollywood sign.
someone brought a bottle of Beam and we all were getting
drunk, already stoned, chilled so high. and I just kept thinking,
man, these California girls are worth it!

the Star Child landed on Rodeo Drive, glittering in flaming glass
beads and purple fake fur.

'damn it!' said Lisa
*'that was one hell of a wave! and we rode it without our sub
scorchers!'*

and someone brought up a case of Haagen Daz, vanilla swiss
almond and we ate it while we all just kept getting higher.

and then there was the tsunami

so we kept on riding the waves

riding the waves, man!
riding the waves!

we climbed aboard a yacht, where the homeless had joined us
smoking grass, singing Beach Boys and eating sushi.
it was the best night ever, my friend ~ in this Califoria town.

people always acting all scared, saying earthquakes are bad.
that all depends on how you ride um!

you gotta ride the waves, dude
smooth
ride the waves
ride the waves

2.

RD held my hand, man. Bob Marley music on the deck.
oranges fell from the grapefruit trees and the water was blue
like candy. we dove into the pool,
we hiked through the canyon.
we rolled down the hills in San Francisco where the flower
children had staked their claim.
we swam off the beach in Santa Barbara.
in San Diego, let the animals out of the zoo.
dropped a match in Palm Springs,   *oh yeah!*
but not before
we spent the night in what once was the house of Lucille Ball,
and we pushed
Liberace's piano down the street.

Oh damn, damn, damn, do I Love Lucy!
and I wish ~ My brother George were here~!

"I hope and pray for another earthquake!
I am from Mississippi and that last one was fun!"

she just kept saying, '*you're crazy, you're crazy!*"

and the streets ran wild. knife fights and crocheted pot holders
for the bad boys making meth. I swear I've never seen such
debauchery.
"STD's are in the crapper. there is a leather party over at
Gene's. they got men strapped-down their since the 1980's and I
think they think they are having fun. their asses pouting, perking
up, worn and ready, pounding, pounding in the sun."

Another EARTHQUAKE!!
and the swimming pools all crack! water sucked up by the cacti
and gutters run the streets. the hot sun is too much and we all
leave town in sports cars and limousines
next stop ~ Disneyland, *man.*

"That damn bus broke down on the 91. That put a dent on the
day. Spent the night in a place called Corona, a flea bag motel
with real goddamn fleas!"

3.

there is a famous artist showing at the Getty, although I can not
remember his name.
lots of food, drinks and stars. they all get excited and they all
dress a-like ~ they all dress the same.
plastic surgery while you wait in line, while your limo circles the
block, and tonight they are giving an award

for

the most

popular

most

beautiful

bastard in town

everyone hopes to win.

*"It's a joke and we all know it, and we all play along, but what
else are you going to do? It's fame, baby, what else can you do?"*

*"that one chick came rolling up in a red carpet, she unrolled,
naked, white as snow. but she looked good baby, she looked
good, and that is the most important part of this life, making
sure it always looks good."*

look good, baby
you
just gotta look good~!

of course the earthquake came to the Getty. we all laughed and
rolled down to the sea. we landed on the island of plastic bottles
and we floated as we watched the world go straight to hell.
with our positive outlook we all knew we had what we needed to
move it along ~ and we would be back before
the new season on HBO.

that chick in the red carpet, now she has her own show. she reads

her lines and stands naked, talking women's rights and we love
her. they all love her, she's going to win that most popular
bastard award

U wait N C.

the next day we head up to Sacramento. we tour the dead almond
trees. the groves are spooky, *man*, the way they stand in the grey.
dead.
all of them, DEAD.
no more bees, *man,* no more bees.

now who will make our salads?
and we need a few more limes.

those almonds were good.
I wish we still had bees.

Bees, Man, Bees.

You remember bees..!

4. (*a royale end*)

standing outside of what was left, watching fires ~ *burn.*
this place was once called Neverland. Peter Pan lived here, but
the earthquake came and left it a gaping hole *straight to hell.*
a messed-up tribute to all cute, innocent, little boys. but there is
peace here, now that Pedo Peter Pan has gone away. years now
without a molestation.

but then too ~ all of the cities had fallen, up and down the coast
and rains fell over the ashes   and   flowers   bloomed.

we all returned to the beach and laid out in the sun. we sang Tom
Petty songs. The Go-Gos, the Mama and the Papas, Tom Jones.
we knew all the words.
                    everyone   every song

*"sing the song about surfing and California Dreamin'. sing it
for this native land that we do love so… and ride a wave, man,
ride a wave!"*

take it far out and up and over and set us safely on the sand.
hike the mountains, play in the snow. we'll plant sunflowers
all the way up highway 101

… plant a garden over looking the surf.

*"that's where I am heading. to a house made of glass. I'll
be happy there, cuz I am happy here. waiting out the clock,
enjoying the sun rise and sunsets, keeping it light, keeping
it free."*

hoping to outlast the next earthquake, *baby* and ride the next
wave.

ride the rain ~ ride the wave, man
if you wanna be free and happy ~ you gotta ride the wave.

West Hollywood

driving down from San Francisco
the text messages, the sexy words that you used
and I keep thinking of your kiss
and the sex that night
and I want you
again

your invatation tenderly wild and passionate
I started packing right away
but when I arrived at
your door
and
you
opened it standing naked
stupid me
with flowers in my hand

you said wide eyed and beautiful

I am so happy you are here.
before you come in, I have something to tell you.

and then I saw them.
the naked bodies behind you
people having sex and laughing without
a care

I really hope you don't mind.
you said
'This is going to be fun.
Everyone here is going to love you.'

I lowered the flowers to my side
dropping them to the ground
I nodded, and stepped forward

A novel

black boots over sandy pebbles
a crew of twenty dragging the lake

I know it is you the words come from
of course my heart knows

cold coffee left on the table
a cup
your name scribbled on the side

restless sleep where I toss and turn in dreams that are
fragments of time

I move through the house
tired mornings pulling out to the world where I see

                                               you

still wanting more

I pace through the city

you
at every corner
lights change color
it is you the words come from
this I know
of course my heart knows

Wrapped in paper

this is my notice.
my paintings wrapped,
under the mat ~ I will place the key.

yesterday my bed remained warm through the
night.
and today,
I woke and drank coffee in this shop, and of course
you remember,
because it was you who walked by with that smile.

> this one declares love
> and that one speaks of passion.

but only you walk by ~ in *s l o w   m o t i o n*

these are my daydreams,
joyful, I move through them.
bash of adventure on this I turn and
again,

in *s l o w   m o t i o n*

You walk by
        with that smile.

unwrap the paper,
call me out.
under the mat ~ you will find the key.

Salt

she gives a moan and then a giggle
wearing a gold lame top and bangled bracelets

her boobs tipping out to the point
I am about to see a nipple

we order dinner and talk and yes, they are
entertaining

her husband talks about money and how much
he makes and the countless ways he likes to spend it

she giggles as she drinks her martini
she winks and tells me that later we will
play

I drink my cocktail and watch the waiter across
the room while I think to myself

you

are a beautiful woman

absolutely

and sexy as hell

but

I do not want to *play* with you later
you alone
or with you and your husband

I won't be in your bed
your hot tub
your mairrage

I want to say it but
I think it instead

the food comes and we all continue talking
all feeling our cocktails and now our wine

again

she speaks of *playing*

he smiles and shakes his head

I see him looking at my arms
I see him wondering if I will thrill her more
I see him getting off on all of this and
I can not help myself

I start *laughing*

desert is a bowl of white cottom candy
she tears it with her red polished nails

he leans in saying no to sugar
he winks

I take a bite

he insists on paying the entire check
he winks

she says let's all go back to the house

I say
what a wonderful dinner, a wonderful evening
I love you both
but
I'd like to return to my hotel

no way
she says
we are going to *play*

the night is young
we will have fun
she says
as we stand

all three of us a little dizzy
all three of us looking the wrong way
we all take a breath and again
I
start *laughing*

she reaches over and takes my hand

Never Neverland

on a little choo-choo train
to a station where creamy cupcakes were served
to the children
                    the obsession
                    the boys
the lust for lollipops and innocence
grooming with candy and trips around the
world
secrets kept behind locked doors where
promises were made then broken by the deviant.
wonderful songs to excite the planet
dance moves to make the girls cry, to wow the men
he took only the little ones in
to his secluded world in his bed
his desires
'I get what I want.'
he would say

and   he   did
little boys sold at Neverland

their innocence forever lost
their promise of the secret held tight
in their tiny heads

and the monster danced on

the young boys panties piled in the corner
the creamy cupcakes and vasoline
Jesus juice at bedtime
to make the boys dream
as the demon takes them over

truth
wins in the end

blessings to the men who were boys who were hurt
by Michael Jackson

2 the Preditor of PYT

as a boy I loved you ~ all my life
I loved you and I understood your damage
this can be a heartless, brutal world
still, there is never a just excuse for
harming a child.

cold and calculated in your style of love
and you told us, informed us knowing
someday it would surely get out
that you were a SMOOTH CRIMINAL
BAD even DANGEROUS

molested myself as a child I also held it
in, knowing it had deep and riding impacts
on who I came to be

so I feel couragous for the victims in
wanting them to be believed
and I no longer listen to you
or care to see your face
this was no small attraction or
miscellaneous mistake
you were calculating even
evil in the love you gave to very
young boys and then took away

you groomed the world and it worked
talent and money your weapon and we
paid you gladly and you lied to us
every single day

I hope your soul is healing and at peace
I hope to never hear or see you again
for your legacy deserves to be tarnished
like the rusty broken down gates of
Neverland.

Now and then

I walk down town to clear my head
to a coffee shop with people, all of us
pretending no one else is around.

gazing in windows my   mind   floating
both sides
        shifting

so often I just get tired and

                wish
it
all would
            end

where is this going
where does it lead

and then
someone will smile or laugh or hand someone
a flower or hold a door or stand up for someone
with integrity
acts of kindness that bring a cloud to my eyes
and I wipe them as my heart follows
        fills
        with
    love for respect and kindness.
that is something we must reveal in our world
everyday
the power of respect and kindness

It is Sunday morning so most streets are quiet
        I walk
    turning the corner
gazing in windows, my mind floating both sides.

In Earnest

you could see your breath,
you could feel it.
I
unzipped my jacket
and sat at the window by
the wall.
my hands
wrapped around the hot
paper cup that
held my coffee.
a fresh
batch
of blueberry scones.
breaking mine in half,
tasting
the dry sweet cake,
I sipped my coffee
warmth to my belly,
I tugged the
scarf
from around my neck.
outside,
the palm trees
just starting to glow
purple as the sun
began to rise

you sitting across the room
striking
your deep good looks
the way you dress
your yoga and pilates.

we both smile a hello
friends only on social media but
not in life
but someday
I hope
I dream

Jesus music Vol. 1

the sandwich was wrapped in wax paper
folded neatly and tucked at the corners.
unwrapped, the rich scent of the roast beef,
sharp cheddar and crisp lettuce.
I took a bite and closed my eyes.

I placed the tangerines in the glass bowl and
lightly washed them with the lemon water
and then
   I tipped
the bowl
spilling the tangerines into the basket to dry.

I pulled the chilled glasses from the freezer and
prepared a bucket of ice.
slicing the fruit with a sharp knife, the sticky
juice covering my hands, I poured the nectar over
the ice into the shaker and snapped down the silver lid.
he
had left a case of Belvedere vodka on the counter
he
was thoughtful like that
his way of saying
    we have plenty, please make more
    lots and
    lots of martinis.

he was standing beside the pool, looking down to the blue
water.

I kept watching him and he kept glancing at me.

I shook the shaker vigorously as I like my martinis cold
and wet with those tiny shards of ice.

I took a long, slow sip, the bite of the vodka, the sweet scent
of the tangerine.

these were good.

I poured another glass and carried them out to the pool
he had Carole King playing on the stereo and he had laid
fuzzy orange beach towels on the benches for us to recline.

he was smiling with his handsome face and the golden
sunshine of sunset
gave him a movie star glow

"Don't leave tomorrow."
he said,
"I like having you here."

and then he downed the last of his martini
dropped his trunks
and dove to the bottom of the pool.

Dukes

that's the moon that tides the heart
and lights the fire.

I need dark walls and whiskey
when I hang my head and my hat from
the heat
or for any reason.

that's the moon that tides the heart
and lights the fire.

the desert sun was back to baking and
my heart was deep in the well and doing
it's best to heal.
I drove to my favorite hideout in Indio and
                    stepped into the darkness
with
those sparkling pink Chirstmas-tree lights leading to neon beer
signs and the faded blue velvet bar stools
with
one
calling my name.

that's the moon that tides the heart
and lights the fire.

I sat and
ordered a Medelo with a shot of Jim Beam.

                 here I could relax
              not a soul would find me.
              here I sit with my wounds
           bleeding into the stillness with no
                explanation to anyone.

light the fire, light the fire!

a good bartender can read a person and this one knew to leave
me alone.

I downed my shot and carried my beer to a booth in the back.

I pulled a pair of blue dice from my pocket
and rolled them with my fingers
felt their poison in my hand and then I dropped them

to

    click

and

     tumble

     on
the

table.

their numbers stopping at 6

the roar of the air conditioning unit on the roof
damnit!

the cracking peanut shells on the floor and the sour scent of
whiskey and beer from the souls who were here before me.

the hollow in my heart
the blood flushing
pulsing through my veins
and suddenly the air conditioning unit
sounds like the twine
engines of a jet plane
falling
falling
to
crash

another beer

quarters ~ songs ~ 20

Merle Haggard and Waylon Jennings, Sturgil Simpson and Al
Green. the Alman Brothers and Elton John.

and I played Ray Charles ~ *Anybody with the Blues*.
                    over and over
                and this cowboy danced…
                        alone
                         til
                         my
                  head felt dizzy
                and my heart felt light;
20 more quarters
I select seven more songs
and
                        this lonely soul
                        kept dancing

I don't care what the truth is in a relationship gone south.
I don't care about who is right and who is wrong.
no two sides are ever on the same in an agreement.
not even in the end.
when it is over.
when hearts are on the sleeve
minds scrambled in pain
who gives a fuck
really
who gives a damn
so much pain and
confusion you can't start over
who gives *a fuck*
really
who gives a damn

a sad sad story
everyone has their own

and

then

other patrons enter the place, the bar becoming busy
so
I tip the bartender

call a cab
and step out to the warm night air

the moon is back
like the night before
seductive and whispering names

on the matchbook
    what I had scribbled:

> *that's the moon that tides the heart*
> *and lights the fire.*

and *finally* ~ the goddamned night felt right

I crawled into the cab and mumbled to the driver
may I please have the windows down, I said,
and take me home

622 warm sands.

A drive in the desert and a shot of Patron

Open the rain

out of focus
shimmers of light as they reflect
from the sequins
purple
blue
orange
the muted haze
of an off balanced image
a woman's face
illusion
she moves in slow motion
perfect skin, radiant smile
full
red
lips
the blue sky
and the rock
walls of this canyon straight up
a wounded bird
falling
down
dizzy
relentless
she sees this and she watches
tears
fill
her
face
the music
ends
as the rain
begins
on a world out of focus

Dark storm looming

he is awake
tired
needing a nap

outside
dark clouds
thunder rolls in a
turbulent sky

stepping from the porch
cowboy hat in hand
Mason
walks to his truck

behind the wheel
he begins to drive

reaching behind the seat
he grabs a rag and wraps his
heart
still the blood ~ a dull flat pain
the sky
turns black
the air turns cold
the truck moves on in the rain, through
his biting confusion, his *rage*

pulling to the side of the road
Mason jumps out *fast*
ripping his shirt from his body
in fear
he strips down as he walks
boots
socks
jeans

jock
left scattered along the asphult
like tumbleweeds in the wind
a flash of lighting in the distance

again
the thunder
again
again
CRACKS the sky
summer rain
cleanse
to calm
to heal
insane
insane
insane
insane
insane
blood
left
on the steering wheel

Way out here

a small house sits in an open desert of white sand
a transparent moon hangs in the morning sky

suddenly
a blast of water
streams
cool me
ease me
take my pain

a shower head sits on a pipe
extending from the parched earth
clean
fresh
cleanse my body
my soul
my mind

a 47 Ford truck
in primer and chipped paint
close to the road
where a black raven waits
fly the sky
from the blast of water
against the jagged terrain

out of gas
stranded
the raven flies
alone
I wait

I should care

she stood
looking around
perplexed

her gaze studied
focused
far off in the distance

"Everything here is so ~ scorched,
white ~ blue
faded lavender ~ lonely."

she said,

"It's like you live on the moon."

In another world

Mason and Angie
at the Hot Toddy Lounge
on the dance floor
slow dancing
under the orange and blue light
as Ray Charles sings ~ *I can't stop loving you.*

they talk about Tommy
Mason's best friend
Angie's man.
he has lied to her and she is hurting
and Mason wants to help make it right

Mason likes Angie
she is one hell of a girl

Angie likes Mason
she wishes…

Mason wishes too…

Vegas wind

the maps flew out the window
somewhere out of L.A.
and Nayer quickly grew upset.

who
needs
a map of Vegas?
you
drive a Tesla
this car can get there by itself.

we stopped in Pasadena for gas
we
grabed an
In & Out burger
and headed back into the night.
the Tesla moving like lightning
through the desert.

we made it to Vegas
where we stayed up for three days
drinking, drugging, gambling, dancing in the clubs
and
when it was all over I said,
"I never want to see Vegas again."

and Nayer laughed, with the top down in the hot sun
the music of Ryan Bringham playing on our way out of town.

Fires bridge

you wanted to meet me
curiosity ~ our fires sparked
crude yet intriguing ~ I wanted to know you
love flowered and the flesh of passion burned.
and then
I saw the dank dark evil side of you.

confused ~ I struggled to make it right
your ugly behavior
my heart broken
mind scrambled
lost

until
that
day
I
      broke
      free

I turned
and I
tossed the torch
to the middle of the bridge
and I walked away
from your damaged heart
while the flames
burned
higher
and you
soon stood watching from the other side
asking why

I could not answer
could not look back
or you would have

found a way
to make my heart stay
deranged excuses
lies
I would have wanted
to
believe

I had to keep walking
away from the heat
allowing the fire
to burn our love
to ash

smolder
smoke
steam
fume
seethe
consume
the
broken
burn
my heart
now
buried
to
waste

Susan Berkley

she wakes in her bed pulling the
sleeping mask from her face
sunshine floods the room
it burns her eyes

she stands pulling on her robe
outside the birds and a lawn mower raging
she crosses the room
stepping out to the landing
then makes her way down the stairs

Susan Berkley is a beautiful woman
her scent of lilac, soft white skin, clear blue eyes
you will not be certain if she is in her fifties or sixties
her elegance will
                    draw you in to stare

down the stairs
                    the lingering ~ scent of lilac

Susan's maid, Celeste
in the kitchen peeling potatoes at the sink
there is an awkward greeting
then Susan announces that she over slept
and *Did Mr. Berkley eat breakfast here at home?*

No Ma'am
He only wanted coffee.

Celeste, I am giving you the rest of the day off.
Of course, with pay.

Susan leaves the kitchen returning upstairs
she stands at the window and watches as Celeste
walks to her car and drives away.

in the master bedroom

Susan digs through the clothes hamper

pulling out her husbands dirty laundry
smelling the shirts
checking the collars
digging the pockets of his pants, *searching, looking*
hoping not to find

searching

in her magnificent home in Pasadena
in her perfect life
a life of devine order
Susan *searches*
knowing what her heart calls her to know

still dressed in her nightgown she sits at her
makeup table
           staring at the framed photo of her husband, Frank

taped to her dressing mirror are photos of
Elizabeth Taylor and Sophia Loren
she is thinking of dying her blonde hair
black

Susan looks at her own reflection
lost somewhere in there
deep in there
deep in despair
deep

lost

For Frank and for Susan

on the phone Susan orders a dozen yellow roses
sending them to the office of her husband, Frank.
knowing ~ Susan ~ knowing
that his secretary will be the first to see them
first to read the card
the white paper card
that reads:

I love You
Frank
Always

Susan

and Susan hopes it ~ *pains* ~ the secretary's heart
she dreams of the secretary in tears
the younger woman
so soft-spoken and kind
so dreamy, she must be dreamy in a man's mind

Susan hates her
she hates that she does
the hate that she has felt this unrest
for
years

and the roses
with their thorns
blood flowing through the yellow
Susan
      each night
            alone

in anguish

Susan makes a second order while on the phone
four dozen white roses with two dozen yellow daisies

having them delivered to herself at her home
she will arrange then for her bedside

watch them as she falls asleep
dream of the world she once knew

dream of white roses and yellow dasies

white roses and yellow dasies

from fields where hearts are free
in places where love is forever
in worlds where happiness
survives

and the card attached
is blank

the card attached of white paper

the card attached says nothing

Alarm

you open the curtains
morning sun blasts
through the window
we glance at one another and both
                    climb
                     out
                    of bed
you to the master bath
I limp down the hall to the other
pissing in the bowl
reflecting in the mirror
looking rested
feeling hollow
feeling
old
trying
to remember…

words from last night
were you happy
did we fight
remember
remember
while pissing in the bowl
was there a fight

I need to know
what
will
set the course for this day

On a good day

I made our breakfast this morning with eggs, mushrooms, bacon and three kinds of cheese. He poured our juice, placed our vitamins on the counter top and talked about the all night rain. How comforting it felt and the splash at the window. Now, a heavy, dense fog, a veil of silver and grey, and we decide that after breakfast, we will take a walk.

In my white robe I sit, looking at this man, in his shorts and scruff of no shave in two days and I think, *'Beautiful.'*
I stand and move around behind him and kiss him gently on the head. He smells sweet, like our pillows. I wrap my arms around him and grip him tight. He tells me the eggs taste good.

Out in Provincetown the fog stays heavy and a light breeze brushes around us and he takes my hand. It just feels right today is what I keep thinking and I wonder why can't more days be like this, and what did we do to start this day off so right?

On the pier, the low moan of a fog horn and his eyes look my way. "Wanna fool around later?" he asks, a smile on his face. "Yes." I say, and I squeeze his hand and I pull him close and I kiss him, and his taste is the one taste I know. It keeps me feeling warm and safe and tells me that he is happy and even with all the bad, there are times that are so damn good.

Seasons

winter in Palm Springs
when the town finally feels alive.
a birthday party on a
Saturday night.
        a mid-century home
        with a green back yard
        a pool ~ a fire pit burning on
the cold desert night.
with
my photographer friend, Gary.
both of us a little high, drinking vodka
cocktails and feeling alright.

"DAMNIT!
It's almost Christmas!'
says Gary

'And another New Year will quickly pass by.
I'm tired of this bullshit!
I want to run across this lovely living-room
trip on that rug…
and send myself ~*sailing!!*
through that plate glass window
at 30 miles an hour!

the man standing behind us hears all that was said
and he starts laughing.

'Do it!'
he says,
'I will glady watch.
This I want to see!'

'Fuckyou'
says Gary.

and we walk outside to the fire.
guys in glamour tops are drinking
from bottles of Goldschlager

       and
inviting guys home for sex on
their living room rug.

'Fuckthis.'
says Gary.

'Yeah, fuckthis.'
I say.

and we leave the party and we
drive to El Marisol
where we eat our favorite Mexican food while drinking
double Margaritas

Then we drive back to his place and we dance to George
Michael, dazzling in trickling blue splashing light glowing
up the pool.
It covers our faces in laughter.

My bed in the Springs

that gentle whiff of
lavender
and I laid in bed for a moment
my eyes
focusing
over
the dark room
where
purple light
crept steady
through an opening in the curtains
across the bedroom floor and up
the wall to the ceiling.

slipping from under the covers
I stood on the cool, slate tile
and walked
down the hallway to the bathroom.

Shirley Horn was singing
throughout the house on a loop I
had started last night.
standing at the stereo
I turned off the power
and the rooms went
silent
to
the birds singing from the garden
out by the pool.

a pot of coffee,
sliced grapefruit,
sprinked with stevia,
back to the guest room
for my robe,
down

the
hall
I looked in to see Dean
sprawled out in his bed
sleeping.
the look of
peace
across his resting,
rugged face.

the mornings

they always hold the tender moments
there is peace in the morings

always the tender moments

Comes from

the pool water was
refreshingly cold
swimming
laps
holding my breath
in
meditation
this would be a good one
a
gush of desert wind
comes from
nowhere
swaying the palms
as they slow dance
above me
I
float
in the water and
listen
to the sounds
the sweet
scent of jasmine
from the plants
that line
the pool
fragrant
hypnotic
seductive
so I linger
in
the water
as long as
I
can

that crazy way

wrapped back in my robe
in a chair with my coffee
I watched the light dawn turn purple, to pink, to gold.
then that voice from behind me…

"Good. You are still here."

and I turn to see him standing, naked, wearing only his
sleepy face.

"I was certain you would take off early, that crazy way that
you do."

"The coffee is good." I say, "Let's take a drive and find
breakfast."

he gave a huge grin, walked to the edge of the pool and
dove in.

Fly the sky

we drove the car up the canyon
at White Water.
niether of us had been there in years.
the air through the pass was
crystal clear, showing
every detail on every
mountain for miles.

I looked out across the mass of turbine towers
that were turning, slowly, energy buzzing with
their huge white blades.
like airplanes
waiting
to take off.

Dean slowed the car and we put down
the windows
the wind sparking our fires to light.

we wound our way up
to the high desert of Yucca Valley.
to a hole in the wall cafe
where we ate eggs, bacon and toast.
the coffee was burnt, tasted sharp,
even buried heavy in cream and sugar.
but we
laughed about it.
Dean sat in the booth across from me.
out the window the view of a Joshua tree.

"Stay in Palm Springs.'
he said.

I spread marmalade on my toast and
handed him a slice across the table.
he took it

thanked me
he took a bite.
"I have lived in Palm Springs for most of my life."
I said,
"Yet it has never felt like home.
I find it elegant and beautiful, but I find so many other
places sincerly exciting."

"I know what you mean."
he said,
"Palm Springs is a unique, comfortable place, but unlike other
places, it dosen't seem to have a soul.
What I like most
is that it is close to L.A.
and it's vibe is laid back when you arrive here from
the city."

I shook my head to agree

"That is the reason I moved here from L.A.
in 88.
To an oasis where you can breath.
I have many memories. Some magical, some lost."

the waitress stopped by and filled our mugs with a fresh round of
bad coffee. Dean flashed me a smile.

"So tell me. When will you go?"

"Soon."
I said,
"Head up north
run free for awhile.
Breath fresh air, bathe in a stream, clear my head,
dance in the wild green meadow."

Dean leaned in across the table and
spoke in a soft husky whisper.

"Take me with you."
he said.

I handed him an unopened pack of marmalade and he gently
brushed my hand
we both took a last look out the window to the desert light
our gaze on that Joshua tree

then I am handed a folded love note
my first one in years

A reluctant goodbye

"I am heart broken that
you are leaving."
he said
pouting his lips like a
child would do.
"And I know all of the
lines that
we will
eventually say.
We will stay in touch.
I will come to see you,
you will come visit me.
That the world
and life
are open before us and we are the
ones who will make it happen or
let it go.

Well, I am saying
that this friendship is important to me,
I love having you around.
The way you talk
and think,
and I hope that when the day comes you
find yourself wanting love
again,

you will
think of me."

Joshua

I looked out the window to the
Joshua tree, perfectly framed in
my site.

it
stood
strong, rugged, beaten.
it's branches twisted and
chewed, gnarled with
time.
it's bark
scarred, and thick from
survival
doing it's damned best
to stay alive,
to keep standing.

"When that day does come."
I whispered softly
and
I kept my eyes on the tree.

Date Palm

back in the car, down the highway
past the Springs, past Rancho Mirage and
Indian Wells, past Indio, to the back roads
that follow the path of the mountain range
to a
stand of date palm trees.
thick
tall and lined in perfect rows
on a dirt path lane.
Dean
pulled the car under the canopy of trees
and we climbed out.
we walked into the grove,
both quiet, listening to the birds,
watching the sunlight
trickle
down
through
the
palm fronds, not quite making it to the earth.

"These groves were once too many to
count, all through these parts."
I said,
"Over the years they have ripped them out to make way
for golf courses and country club housing.
When I first started coming out here in the eighties,
for all of it's style, Palm Springs had a wild side that
I miss."

we walked
farther into the trees
talking about future plans and dreams.
Dean kept his phone in his
back pocket and would let
it ring.
he was a master at giving you his full
attention,

in caring what you had to say.

I watched him walking in his blue tank top
as he kept looking up into the
green branches
and I suddenly realized that
he had become a sort of hero
of mine.
it always feels good to meet people
that you admire, respect, the joy
that comes when you are face to face
with integrity.

he stopped walking but kept
searching
the
tree tops above

"I wish there were dates on these trees
right now."
he said,
"Being in the middle of this maze
really makes me want one."

I took my cowboy hat from my head and looked back towards
the car that we had strayed so far from.

"Have you ever had a date shake?"
I asked and he shook his head.

"No, but I want one."

he licked his lips and rubbed his hands together.

"There is a place in Indio. We'll stop on our way
home."
I said, and we started to walk again.

"We are alone, just like you wanted, no one else around
as far as we can see."

we both turned and looked in all four directions.

only date palms and bursts of sunlight and shadows of
the trees.

"Stand still."
I said,
"Close your eyes and you can feel the
presence of the palms as they are planted around us.
*their life force feels that we are here and they know that we
came to see them."*

      we both stood perfectly still for several moments.

"I can feel them."
he whispered.

I opened my eyes and there he stood, eyes closed,
smiling, his hands out stretched, taking in the energy.

"We've made new friends."
he said.
and he opened his eyes, walked over and shook my
hand and we both started laughing.

NIght cap

back in Palm Springs
we picked up a reuben sandwich
from Sherman's Deli and we took it
home to share.
we walked Luke through the winding
streets of the Movie Colony as the sun
fell back
behind the mountain.

after a little TV
we laid on the lounges out by the pool.
the blue light
trickled up through
the water.
Dean fell asleep. I covered him
with a blanket and I
pulled one over Luke as well.
I laid there
looking up
at the
stars,
the soft light
dancing over the palms.
a deep
breath, a stretch, and a yawn.
Shirley Horn
sang softly in the air
floating over
a great sense of
gratitude and peace.
the intoxicating
scent of jasmine.
with
my good friend
sleeping on the chair beside me.
my dog curled up on my lap and
and - my - eyes
growing - heavy.

Read me

the box, the suitcase, the bag…
I am drifting along the pool
out above the water
don't let me drown
feel my need
hear my call
save me
just
this
one
time
slip the box into the bag into the suitcase

fish my story out of the pool
and
read
me

Your love note in my hand

Dean kept his key on a silver dollar key chain from
the Bellagio Hotel Casino in Las Vegas, Navada.

I open the front door
turn off the alarm and
turn on the music.
Antonio Jobin's
    WAVE
fills the house ~
It's rhythm rattles the walls
              floods the pool
          waters the palms and
                  spills out
                      over
the streets of Palm Springs ~ where it
then races
      down
          quietly
            to the gutter.

I pull the folded paper from my pants,
take off my clothes, I drop the paper into the
chilled blue water ~ where the music notes and
confetti break free
          from my
              body and *float off ~ singing to the sky.*

I swim down to the bottom
forced to
look back to the
          ghost on the shore
and the dreams of that world are where I
slumber *and the nightmares cry out from the soul.*

a tangerine tonic
over crushed ice

unfolding the paper note
I take it with me
down
to the bottom
and I
float it
over the pull of the drain
It's white pulp turns translucent
then to
an electric shade of green
reminding
of a painting
hanging lonely
in a mid-century modern filled with rage.

a spin of the paper in the water and the painting so
clearly I see.
lime green mixed in a mason jar
over white ribbons of a road
leading off
to adventures, laid down layer after layer of
the wickedly wonderful shocking schemes.
glaze
and then
the crisp teal colored tie
around the neck of the handsome bank teller
and the sparkle he carries in his eyes.
I wonder if the waitress at the cafe is happy with
her tips for the night and if she will
be finding love in a new town soon
all of us drifting
down the drain
                the love note fading to white

Changing Jobin

the gentle approach is perfectly
fitting
perfectly fitting
into the night
my hands on Dean's robe
I wrap myself in
then walk once around the pool

I pull the sheets down in the guest room and turn off the lights
all except for that prussion blue lava-lamp left on in the hall.

the paper is drying on the lounge chair
shifting reality
closer to the moon

at 4 AM
I swim to the bottom
where I glance back to see once more that ghost of you and I am
persuaded to abandon all hopes, my dreams of that world where
the gypsy has told me I will slumber clearing in cloudberry

no man tolerates this wild and wooly…
UP
then DOWN
then
OVER

The Tropicale

stepping into the Tropicale
Palm Springs
the night air swirling around
through the pink
the green
the ginger rum taste
with each swallow
and he
as if from the island
steps up while I dine at the bar
a heart of gold
heavy spanish accent
and I say   yes
you may put my number
in your phone

would you like another?
the bartender asks
I crunch my ice
and I say
no

I leave alone
back to my apartment
naked in my bed
I drift
way
back
to a time we are making love
in the backyard where the cold
Florida rain pours over us both
as we gasp for air through our
desperate kisses
and in the power of this
I toss and I turn and I wake from
the dream
only this was not a dream

it was a memory

out of bed
           I take a walk in the early
light
a wet fog   hangs
about the mountain
so rare for Palm Springs
the stars in the sky
the California sun not yet risen

I wrap the blanket around my shoulders
release the bouquet of tiny forget-me-nots
and as my feet dangle
                         above the carpet
of the purple flowers
I realize
this is not a memory but a dream
and I think of how it takes a lot to know a
man but not really
it's not so hard to understand.

and for you
new love
you have my number now
in your phone

and I dream of your touch
knowing
your kisses must be wildly magic

Black Roses

oh fuck but you play the ace of spades like the devil
you know the horror story you toss my way
the twisted abuse that your ego is unable to claim
no perfect triangle job say you born to worship
then
stay down there and prove your passion
your commitment your worth
and you do, you can
take my breath away
and beg me to over power you again
blind fold
tie you down
and please do it again and I do
your weeping tears your begging for more your complete
satisfation
all this is tossed away spit upon as your feet hit the floor
and you return the cold and wicked asshole you know how to be
why?
in cries to all of heaven, why?
I twist you down but always in love
never so far as you request and say you deserve
you must have that psychotic, that monstrous pain
the unhappy ending most every fucking day and night
black roses and disapproval and lies
you rip a cowboy's mind across the room and insist on a bloody
heart
You've got to love me!
you cry
You've got to fuck me!
and I do and I do and I say What the fuck?!
You are going to lose me, I say
up over you, climbing the headboard and telling you
the stories you want to hear
but all of them of love and with care never do I disrespect
I'll rough and tough-boy you better than the rest…
but by God I am for real
my passion is for you if you can fucking respect that

but you're lost in fear of losing me dear and black roses fill your
dark heart
disapproval is your middle name
and black roses are your only game
dirty smelly flowers left rotting on the floor
tell me you love me and that you want more
fooled by games and black roses, stems and thorns ripped across
my skin, my crown
and the confusion as you destroy the best man in town
the real deal, the love of your life
and you piss it away each and every day and most every fucking
night I pack my bags and I walk down the road
and your hammer smashes what remains
coarse ugly words that no other would dare say
hate and loss and pain
chase me away and ask for my return and I do
in my belief that this game won't play, will somehow pull
through
Let's try red roses for once, I plead
NO they must be black, must be filled with poison and pain
if you won't do it get someone in here who will
what kind of sick bastard says that to the love they claim real?
you wanted a real man
you got one
now show up motherfucker like I do
you shame me, guilt me, tell me the places I am wrong
then in bed I hold you and close all night long
used me, tricked me, drugged me
sex with another in the next room
that promise of love turned to horse shit and mud
rolling dice of confusion gasoline dread
black roses across the cold, muddy bed
I bring the rainfall blessed to cleanse our fights
you bring the bull dogs to rip us apart each night
poison my cock saying no other will have it
melt it down and choke and chew on it
black roses say you but I wanted red
passion and fire and love in my bed
black roses you bring and say please don't leave me
black roses and lies and your work to decieve me
actions speak louder then words on this level
and you play the ace of spades like the devil

part three

Are those roses or are those oysters?

And I will start over from here.

They say the hills are once again green and that the oaks trees
are filled with life.

Becoming Phoenix

Buz

To wake from a dream of rain on the dock
by a lake with thousands of birds and moths and
multi-colored bettles filling the air.

and I wake.

The body approaches

say this resembles the form of a new start
it is difficult for me to recognize

the endless swinging articulation
where apples smell sweet and their juice
runs down your arm

so I hand you my handkerchief and you wipe your skin clean

and that cloth you returned
I now keep treasured, beneath my pillow

Promise me

oh you birds with your berries
flutter the trees
knowing as well as we do
the changing view it at hand
and still
you sing your song
so pretty

up
from the fire
becoming phoenix
stories
of children who
love
who
wish to live with laughter
and light

you
birds
in the sky
are the promise to last for the
lovely children
                        please please
do not drink the water
of ours
for we have killed the bee
and the moths are
crying
as the roses
sob
please bring us back
to
life

Slane

I think about all of this
it is
winding down.
fed up, I move on to something new.
to a place of freedom where I am able to breath.

driving to the coast I head north
spending weeks in Seattle where the rain washes
a good part of my brain.

you know I know
I have good reason to shut you out
a sharp bit of metal that cuts your edge cutting deeper
taking from me your disease

toxic   you

rain on me skies of Seattle
cleanse my wounds
                        tide me to the salt waters
of sea
keep me healing under dark skies
refuse the sun

I need the shade of grey for comfort.
I need the darkness to heal.

Agave

I stepped out of the car and roses scattered to the ground
I moved on to the garden with the wrapped gift in my hand
music was playing over tree tops and
champagne bottles were opened as I made my
way to the pool
and from somewhere in the darkness
your whisper called my name.

Summer girl

from the bed where you
left me
in the darkest night
I see

       your blue dress
the moon shining out in the garden
where I look for you still
through the glass
            panes of praised music and dance
my heart in your hand
you ran
now
out dancing
and the moon has gone   too
out the window tonight

             stumble
          from inside this lonely heart
from the bed where you
left me

the clock ticks on the nightstand
I turn it to the wall, a pillow over
the light and now in the darkness

          I wish the return of moonlight

on the cold sheets where you left my mind
                to shine in the garden
                    where you
                      return
       in your glowing blue dress

On this night

I walk across the sand, through the woods
to a cabin where there are rose petals across a velvet
covered bed

in the yellow moonlight and in the shade of sweet pine
I will sleep here, alone ~ in a gentle dream

Indian blanket

highways down from Montana, listening to Bruce Springsteen
the entire way. Early morning coffees, afternoon rains.

arriving in New Mexico where the massed clouds in the blue
billow of dancing white and the scent of the pine gives a cool
green stare.

standing out in the yard
driven by curiosity
free from the hunger
at the cabin
by the river
finally home

and this whisper flows down through canyons into my
heart
through my longing for you

pine forests
sweet flowers
orange and yellow
in your
brown hair
I hold on to these memories ~ as so many smolder
in the ash
but those flowers
once of you
are here with me

everywhere

Rockwood

an olive branch replaces forget-me-nots
and even that ~ I let go

hearts wrapped in velvet cloth with the red dripping
through
to the streams of the moutain

where thunder clouds drift and call
gentle in a tone that sounds of you
trembles in air through me

view ~ across the valley
from the edge of a cliff
this life
the end of love that I taught you so well
hold your breath close
wait
and do it again
and as you do
          think of me
ingrain me to your patterns
of light
of lust
as I do
map the stars for you

      begging the mother of nature to heal me

      allow me to be free

for this new start is breaking
   this new start is for the birds who sing in the tree
without all the worry

how I dream to fly like the falcon
someday once again
             to flly

From Black Lake

the highway out from the ranch
dusty road through pine where a murder of crows
call my name

a bottle of champange opened, between my legs
the windows down, a cassette tape of Tanya Tucker's
Riding Rainbows.

sunday morning the sun shines through clear tangles that were
webs
I'm thinking that it's illegal to drive and drink and drunk but I'm
feeling rebal and wild in my oats.

the medicine drive through Eagle's Nest
dropping down into Red River
hiding the now empty bottle under my seat

this craving for a steak at Texas Red's but they won't be
open for hours

pulling into the Riverside, I rent a cabin
spread out on the bed
play a round of cards
order a pizza and fall asleep

I wake as early evening sends a chill down over the valley
change shirts and head out to the Motherlode

a band plays
            I drink beer and I talk to a lady
up from Oklahoma City

she talks about a cold summer this year
I agree

beyond small talk ~ I am just not in the mood

I walk back to my cabin watch an old episode of Columbo and I fall asleep

this is my life, I think - when I wake at two in the morning in the darkness

not so bad but.... I don't know.

too much time on my hands but not enough time left in life

the quiet space I like

in this world never lonely at all
but still
the thought of love and that would be...

something.

the next morning I check out of the cabin and drive back to the ranch in Black Lake.

the empty champage bottle still under my seat

The poet beside my bed

you hate him don't you
he is telling everyone that you do
the voice came from the dark corner

I do not hate him
I said
but the degree of broken was killing us both
there was love
but there was nothing more I could do

he stepped forward and I could see him
watching me
the glow of his light
this man
who had somehow slipped back into my room
his musky scent reminding me
my sleepy brain dizzy
as
I struggled to see that he continued to hold

my leather bound book
his tricks of retrieval mocking my attempts of
keeping him at bay

standing beside my bed
never once taking his eyes off of me
he waited

there were low whispers
a chill in the room
wild
there was wild

as I noticed the open window
I pulled my blanket up tight
he closed his eyes
while the flutter of paper
like white moths circling the flame

you gave your permission
he said
the gift you gave to me

your thoughts free to the passing of time

the window closed
the pages stopped turning
the heat smoldered deep in his eyes
his thumb brushing past
paper and pain
and then
quiet
in the room

the red flame went out
I could not see him but could hear him breathing
and then his low voice rumbled gently from the darkness
of the corner

all of this is a part of you
the pain, the love, the roses, their thorns
forget none of it
embrace each bit of it
be thankful for the road at all

and then

he was gone

I climbed from the warm covers for a glass of water
and crossed the creaking floor
past the curtains holding the night

in the next room I sat in a chair
wrapped warm in my blanket
tears gone
I fell alseep

when I woke the next morning
soft sunlight beaming through the curtains
squinting through blinds

I felt thankful

I felt thankful

that I could be in this space

that I could feel the sun
that I could feel the heat

thankful
for the passing night
for the new day

About the Author

AC Calloway is a painter and poet living in Montana and New Mexico. He enjoys spending most of his time in nature and on the open road.

The Broken Burn is his second collection of poetry.

Follow AC, at:

ACCALLOWAY.COM

Book design and grapfics by A.C. CALLOWAY
copyright 2019 A.C. CALLOWAY

51355780R00151

Made in the USA
Lexington, KY
02 September 2019